California Medieval

California Medieval

Medieval

Nearly a Nun in 1960s San Francisco

Dianne Dugaw

Schaffner Press

Excerpts from this work were originally published in different
form in the following publications:
"God's Knitting Needle" was published in *Mount Hope Magazine*, 10 (2016); "Material
Calling" appears in *Pensive: A Global Journal of Spirituality & the Arts*, 5 (2022).
Biblical quotes are from the Catholic Douay-Rheims translation (1582; 1609-10).

Hang On Sloopy
By Bert Russell and Wes Farrell
Copyright © 1964, 1965 by Morris Music Inc., Sony/ATV Music Publishing LLC
and Sloopy II Inc. in the U.S.
Copyright Renewed
All Rights Reserved Used by Permission
Reprinted by Permission of Hal Leonard LLC

Cover and Interior Design: Jordan Wannemacher
Cover image: Courtesy of Adobe Stock
Manufacturing by The Maple Press.

Library of Congress Control Number: 2024939393

Paperback ISBN: 978-1-63964-054-6
Ebook ISBN: 978-1-63964-056-0
Epdf ISBN: 978-1-63964-057-7

While this is a work of non-fiction, the author has changed names
of certain characters out of respect for those individuals' rights of privacy.

Contents

California Medieval

How Not to Meditate

EVERY MORNING, MEDITATION TIME at Mount Alverno comes early, just after Sister Agatha, the Postulant Mistress, rouses us at 4:30 a.m. with the light of Christ. Hollering midway between a shout and a chant, she marches down the hall and into our rooms: "LU-U-U-U-men CHRIS-ti." And the required reply from each of us, however half-hearted: "DE-E-E-E-o GRA-A-A-tias." It takes me a matter of minutes to get up and dress, so I usually have time to go outside and walk the roadway that rings the top of the mountain. Early birds and rabbits hop around in the brush. Dawn seeps up behind the mountains south and east of San Jose and dapples the tide flats at the end of the Bay, that bit by bit shimmer into view.

Meditation happens in the half hour or so before the bells ring for Lauds, which we start singing at 5:30 before the Mass at 6:15. The chapel is swimming in shadows with a few single lights brightening the back walls. Sister Delphine's Pine-Sol treatments leave a sharp tingle jumping up my nose, along with traces of the other cleaning and gleaming and polishing agents she directs us to rub into the floor so it shines for the Lord. Footsteps tiptoe on the slick marble, rosaries rustle, and knees genuflect beside the pews as one by one the whole community arrives, each going to her place.

We postulants—brand new, aspiring nuns—take our places on the north side, in one arm of the cross that makes up the architectural design of every Catholic church I've ever seen. We face the sanctuary and the altar in the center. The novices, one and two years ahead of us in their vocation schedules, fill up the pews to the side of us in the big chapel's longer main part in the east, going back to the tall double-doors under the organ loft. On the other side of the sanctuary, in the arm of the cross on the south side opposite us, sit the professed sisters who have taken their vows.

The hanging sanctuary lamp flickers in its red glass. Me, I'm not very adept yet. It's not clear to me at this point what should happen. So, I look at the wriggling flame in the lamp, enjoy its swirlings. How do air currents make it all the way down into that glass cone to tickle the flame into jumping and dancing?

What most distracts me from edification comes with watching the professed nuns across the way. The superiors and administrators of Mount Alverno Convent, Motherhouse of the western U.S. province of the Franciscan Sisters of Christian Love and Atonement—Mother Priscilla, Sister Emmeline, Sister Ursula, and Sister Monica—seem just as competent with meditation as with all their business. They sit up straight, read a bit from some meditation book or maybe the Bible, close their eyes purposefully, then focus—spot-on—right to the point. Perhaps they're letting God in on how they'd like to keep everything going smoothly today: with the call to the bishop about financing the province; with organizing the annual retreat for Mount Alverno's more than one hundred nuns and would-be nuns; with scheduling the transfers of nuns across the province from one school or hospital to another; with the call to the mechanic about selling the old cars and replacing them with new models; with instructing their classes here with us or at one of the Catholic colleges nearby; with how to get help with whatever things worry people who are in charge of everything.

The cooking and cleaning and laundering sisters and old retirees have a whole different approach. I'm busy wondering which one is going to fall asleep and keel over first as, one by one, on the far side across the expansive sanctuary, they start to succumb. Leading the way, as it were, Sister Martina nods. The heavy black-lensed aviator glasses that cover a lot of her face and help with her bad eyes catch the light and cast weird beams on the ceiling. Her veiled head wobbles and tips to the left. She's broad and planted, so she's actually not going to do more than lean and tilt. Next, little Sister Epiphania slumps to one side and drapes herself and her bony arms dramatically over the edge of the oak pew. Her glasses perch at a rakish angle off her narrow nose. Sister Regina, who runs the laundry and races about all day from one huge washer or dryer to the next, smiles with her eyes closed. After a while she shakes herself awake once or twice, then finally slides off in the other direction, avoiding a collision with Sister Epiphania. Sister Delphine is as solid and in control in meditation as she is wielding one of her giant revolving-brush polishers down a newly waxed hallway. With her eyes closed, you'll never know if she's asleep or just listening more intently. There's no tipping or even head-nodding with her.

There's no head-nodding for me, either. One part of my mind is busy with imaginary wagers over the little old nuns across the way, more or less picturing bowling pins. As I look around, I have to wonder how this convent life is going to work out. Where am I headed here? When the bells ring for Lauds, my heart jumps in surprise.

Material Calling

AS A FRANCISCAN NUN, you've hardly any earthly complications to distract you from your immaterial calling. No clothes to speak of, just a couple of identical brown habits. No books of your own beyond your breviary and maybe a Bible and a missal for Mass—and I brought my guitar and banjo from home. No knick-knacks or mementos, let alone shelves to put them on. Standard-issue everything, and not much of that. In addition, a blanket of silence wraps this spare world from morning till night—almost no talking anywhere most of the time.

The entrance door to any convent opens onto floor polish—lustrous wood or tile and that not at all faint scent of soap and polish. Mount Alverno Provincial Motherhouse for the Franciscan Sisters of Christian Love and Atonement fits the pattern perfectly—really exceeds it in olfactory pungency, what with Sister Delfine's masterful Theater of Motherhouse Cleaning Operations. The seemingly endless corridors whisk into gleaming and piquant circles of shine, their surface reflecting the surroundings like a mirroring stream anytime a window is near.

The Provincial Motherhouse is a recent addition to the top of this mountain. Bright white and up-to-date, the rangy complex extends out from a vaulting high-roofed chapel and bell tower. At the front of this large central building are offices, classrooms, parlors, patios, visiting halls and guest rooms. At the back side on the main floor are two refectories for meals on opposite sides of an industrially equipped kitchen. Beneath, on the floor below, are extensive laundry facilities next to a big garage, delivery loading docks, and, a short distance away, a few small storage sheds. From the chapel and the center of the main building, long and narrow extensions reach in opposite directions: one to the south lined with cells for the professed sisters, and another to the north for the novices and postulants. Unadorned, ascetically white, and starkly angular, the whole place says: lift your eyes aloft to the heavens; keep your mind in the clouds and off the details. But such a clean-sweep can—paradoxically—make every little thing pop with tangible energy. Take smells for example.

If you didn't come in the front to the parlors and offices of Mount Alverno, but rather walked the circular drive around to the back side, it's not so much corridors and piney floor polish. This morning, I've finished the digging and weeding that Sister Noella assigned me on garden duty. I'm out back putting away my shovels and hoes, with a nice stretch of time to myself before chapel and the chanted procession of Psalm 50 down the halls to the refectory for lunch: "Have mercy on me, O God, as thou art rich in mercy."

A stone's throw from the shed where I stow my tools, Sister Regina's giant, infernally hot open-air laundry-room sends out billows of steam. Where I stand, the air sizzles with laundering. Smells of spicy-soaping, steamy-rinsing, bleached and burnt-baking cottons, wools, denims, nylons, and linens fly through the air, as laundering stuff makes its way from one gleaming and growling machine to the next. Along with varieties of cleansing and searing cloth, the air circulates a medley of smells from the hot, roiling metals that are bouncing, rinsing, spinning, tossing, clamping, and pressing item after item, from dirty and rumpled to clean, smashed, and smooth.

Careful to remain below the radar so I can enjoy my meandering free time, I turn the back corner by the laundry, past the loading docks where trucks full of furniture, food, soaps, office supplies, or who knows what periodically pull in and deliver their requisitioned wares—along with stinging smoke and carbon monoxide chugging from their idling engines.

In the convent garage around to the side, with its door panels open for the day, slimy spots on the cement floor emit trickles of gasoline and other petrol and car-wax products that bring to mind service stations. Last month I was on garage duty and worked on the fleet of cars, checking their oil and gas, washing them inside and out, sweeping and tidying the whole place. Open any car door here and out floats an almost-sweet scent of vinyl seats and plastic knobs and buttons that hovers aromatically with the petrol. Or, if it happens to be a door of the convent's grand Buick, a smoother, dusky scent of leather, even a hint of small handles made of actual wood.

The provincial autos line up in the garage ready for use if needed: the magisterially silver Buick sedan that Sister Ursula might drive to a meeting with a prelate or to take Mother Priscilla to the airport; two nondescript greenish Chevy station wagons, which Sister Monica might take to teach at the Dominican college nearby, or a designated novice might drive for a novitiate outing or to ferry one of the professed sisters to a dental appointment; two smaller Ford two-doors—one blue and one brown—for any medical or dental trips for novices and postulants; and at the far end, the tiny and miscellaneously-assigned gray Fiat—a little mushroom parked alongside a row of stately garden shrubs.

One floor above the garage, Sister Marietta's kitchen bangs and whirrs with busy sounds of lunch preparation. Sister Marietta was my favorite nun back home in first grade, when she was stationed at St. Mary's mission school up north on the prairie. We've had kind of a reunion here. Now, whiffs drift out the windows and doors of her kitchen almost any time of day. A huge slow fan from the high ceiling wafts out billowing smells of yeasty bread, tasty beef bits crackling in giant pans, sizzling onions and peppers spitting in grease, along with the smooth salty sniff of potatoes. Rising to the ceiling and high windows and back, random floating hints of cooking can flit their way down otherwise odorless hallways—to one side, past the somber provincial business offices; to the other, toward the novitiate classrooms, maybe even ascending pristine stairs toward the chapel.

A sliding door down along one hallway, when shut tight, effectively bars kitchen smells from the enclosed patio. Opened, the door leads to where Sister Noella's prize roses fill the air with aromatic esters above their garden beds. At the near end, the petals of huge pinkish-white blooms, big as oranges, let off an almost-citrus scent that whispers for a moment and then disappears. Further on, crimson clusters throw off something deeper and sweeter, a juicy ripe apple or red wine. At the far end, draping from their trellis, pale Cecile Brunner buds quiver in the slightest wind and blow their savory cinnamon under the eaves of the alcove. The tangy sweetness sometimes even trails out the patio's far door to drift down the staid hallway past the provincial offices of business, accounting, and administration.

Each hallway eventually reaches a stairway to the chapel. I go up the novitiate stairs and enter from the side. Clouds of frankincense from the morning High Mass still hang below the vaulted ceiling these many morning-hours later. Smoky wisps catch sunbeams above the pews. I inhale a heavy leftover dose of the sacred smoke. Sneeze a few times. Cough. Then head to the tall back door of the chapel that opens onto the high part of the mountain top.

The south end of San Francisco Bay glimmers below distant peaks of snowless mountains. I breathe deeply. Leaving the wide outdoor entrance-way to the chapel, I stroll down to the eucalyptus grove along the cliff at the edge of the property. Wend around among the prickly junipers, twiggy grasses, varieties of cactus, and the occasional web-covered tarantula hole. Look out over the hum of urban California below. Breathe again. Sniff the gentle menthol in the air beneath the young trees after last night's rain.

Lifting, Narrowing, and Frowning

I HAD BEEN IN the convent only three days when Sister Agatha walked me down a dark hallway past classrooms to Sister Mechtilde's studio-office. Outside, the afternoon blew breezy and California-warm. Even indoors, the chirping of birds around the bell tower followed us. At the end of the corridor, I spotted two small upright pianos through the half-glass pane of the closed office door. They reminded me of Sister Marie Celine's piano-teaching room at St. Mary's—one of my favorite places. Sister Agatha rapped briskly.

"Y e- e- s,   S i s T e r," a contralto voice responded, *Lento*, from the other side of the door.   "D o.   L e T.   Y o u r S e l F.   i N." Precisely chiseled consonants clipped each syllable.

Music had gotten me through everything in my life so far. From second grade on, if I was worried about my homework or sickly younger siblings, I could play piano, and my mind would ease off. I never liked game-times at school with kids yelling and bullying each other. By fifth grade I'd slip into the piano practice rooms, and get through recess fine. When everybody in our big family got mumps but me, I played soft Mozart (while

Mom took people's temperatures, gave out the aspirin, and made chicken soup). Playing music made it possible to get through even the worst of times like when my colt and my little brother died.

At home and at school, I played the piano with Sister Marie Celine as my teacher, winning contests and even accompanying the high school choir by sixth grade. At chapel and later for church, I was the organist and, with her coaching me, I was already playing for First-Friday Benediction in fifth grade. Guitar and banjo, I picked up on my own without lessons, and played on every possible occasion with my family or alone, especially old songs and sad ones like "Red River Valley" and "Irene, Goodnight." We sang a lot at home, us older kids adding harmony with Mom. On arrival, my guitar and banjo got parked here in their cases in a closet down the hall. Immediately, I located the various pianos at Mount Alverno: the sturdy uprights in this studio, a Wurlitzer spinet in the front parlor area, and a nice baby grand in the downstairs recreation room.

Sister Mechtilde manages all the chanting and liturgical music at Mount Alverno. She directs the choirs and singing groups, purchases any hymnals or sheet music for the convent and supervises where they're kept and used, plays the organ for liturgies, and is the instructor for anybody who wants to study piano or organ. Though I'm pretty accomplished, I have in mind to learn more and to be sure I can make music here every chance I get. How can I be at home here otherwise?

Sister Agatha opened the door as directed, and we entered the little office. Against my chest, I held tight the prized books of piano music that I brought with me: Bach two- and three-part inventions, Haydn and Mozart sonatas, Chopin waltzes and preludes, a wild toccata by Khachaturian.

"G o o D.   D a y.   S i s T e r.   A G a Th a.   W h a T. M i g h T.   Y o u.   B e.   N e e D i n G?" Through her pursed lips, Sister Mechtilde's phrases sounded as measured as an oven-timer, the kind you wind and set ticking. Every consonant landed with a TOCK.

Sisters Mechtilde and Agatha, in almost comical counterpoint, reviewed in detail when an already structured convent day might accommodate piano and organ lessons. Intermittently, Sister Mechtilde dabbed her lips with ChapStick. Every few phrases, her pale eyes peered through half-inch-thick, unrimmed glasses to squint in my direction. Doubts began to creep into my mind.

How old was she? Pretty old.

With her thin, gray eyebrows lifting, narrowing, and frowning by turns, she weighed possibilities and counter-possibilities. Having risen from her small desk when we entered, she stood stiff as a ruler. Her fingers fidgeted the edges of a meticulously ironed scapular—the outer part of the habit that draped down from her shoulders—as if to flatten each thread to greater evenness. Her low voice murmured a range of options for lesson times—some late mornings and afternoons, piano in the studio, organ in the chapel loft. As she spoke, minutely detailing possible accommodations with pluses and minuses for each, her upper lip scarcely moved. I looked down at my feet. My musical future at Mount Alverno was dimming.

My eyes surveyed the shiny white linoleum floor. Beneath the brown of Sister Mechtilde's Franciscan habit, two granny shoes gleamed, polished and buffed almost as gleaming-black as patent-leather. I lifted my head (sighing). Through the tiny window above Sister Mechtilde's desk, the junipers jumped with birds. Many years ago, a dark and difficult metronome entered the convent to became a nun who took the name "Sister Mechtilde."

I've been here long enough—more than a month—to see that day-by-day at Mount Alverno is a kind of timeless time of cycles and repeating rhythms. But, as I go on, I can't help but bump and stumble at the tick-tocking of Sister Mechtilde.

Morning Watch

I love them that love me:
And they that in the early morning watch for me,
Shall find me.

(PROVERBS 8:17)

At morning's first start you can slip out
　　the farther door toward the crest of the hilltop.
　　　　Walk the dim road that circles toward the cliffs.

A breeze tickles the tall grasses alongside,
　　in front of the junipers and scrub oak.

Overhead glimmers a smattering of stars.
　　Below, only a faint hum from cities and highways
　　　　stretched out to the wide edge of the Bay
　　　　　　in a twinkling carpet of light.

At the cliffs
    where the mountain drops
        to tree tops far beneath,
            find the smooth, flat rock
                under a small eucalyptus.

Sit there.
Smell the bark.
Hear the leaves rattle
    as ground birds begin their day.
        Wonder about everything.

Light slowly climbs the eastern sky
    and edges with lavender-gray, then pink, then crimson,
        the distant crags of the high mountains.

Watch a corduroy sheen of rainbow colors find
    and shimmer the shallows and salt flats
        of the Bay's far-away waters.

Wait for the sun
    to sliver up behind the peaks,
        a giant lifting the day.

Ribbons of Time

ON ARRIVAL AS A postulant at Mount Alverno Motherhouse, you receive your breviary—the book of prayers for chanting the Hours of each liturgical day—and start learning how to place the book's colored ribbons. Many times a day, you'll reposition them for the next Hour of prayers a while later. Sister Agatha the Postulant Mistress coaches you, together with one of the first-year novices. The psalms and prayers and readings go back-and-forth between a given liturgical Hour for a particular day of every week—Sunday, Monday, and so on—and what's for only one specific day of the year—say, Christmas or the feast of Saint Francis. You have to flip through your pages frontwards and backwards to keep on top of your praying while you're busy at it eight times a day.

I'm used to thinking about the different feasts and saints, and finding their prayers and readings in my missal. Back home, my dad and I went to Mass almost every day at the mission church, and every night when the whole family said the rosary together before dinner, he read from the Bible and the life-story of the saint for the day. But at Mount Alverno, the day's Hours are a whole different ball-game—like going from rookie to pro.

Every Monday morning's chanting of the Hour of Lauds in the chapel begins this way: First, you start where your red ribbon marks the page for the opening Antiphon: "Incline unto my Aid, O God." And its reply, "O Lord, make haste to help me" (an apt plea for how you're feeling on your first day). Then on to the psalm: "O God my God: to thee I watch from the Morning Light."

As the year moves through its seasons, the Divine Office—the liturgy of psalms and readings during each day—organizes the passing of all Hours for the days, weeks, and seasons. While your red ribbon is marking the Hours of a day of the week, your blue ribbon goes to the place in the breviary that marks the year's seasonal cycle of psalms and chants. If it's Christmastide, you'll chant how "The Root of Jesse has Budded out, a Star is risen from Jacob." As the weeks go into Lent and Easter, the blue ribbon moves along, marking stages of the life of Jesus remembered once again each year: "Our Lord has reign'd, he has put on Beauty. Alleluia; our Lord has put on Strength, and girded himself. Alleluia, Alleluia."

That's not all there is to it. Interspersed through the seasons marking the events of the Christ story, other celebrations have to be chanted about. Use your yellow ribbon to follow the calendar for these additional feasts such as the Immaculate Conception of Mary (December 8th) or her Assumption into Heaven (August 15th): "Who is She, that comes forth as the Morning Rising, fair as the Moon, elect as the Sun, terrible as the Front of an Army set in order of Battle?" And the rousing reply: "Thanks be to God."

Then, along the way, further ribbons track the daily calendar for still other saints and sacred events big and small, with apt psalms and prayers in the liturgies for each of them—feasts of saints like Joseph of Cupertino or Joan of Arc, the feasts of Our Lady like her Apparition at Guadalupe, the beheadings and deaths of different martyrs, the dedications of important churches, and so on.

Each feast has generalized parts as well as particular psalms and prayers.

Now, with the yellow ribbon on the particulars, use your green ribbon to mark the general categories: those prayers and readings for all the feasts of Mary, major and minor, and those for any virgin, martyr, apostle, confessor, or doctor of the church with prayers celebrating or calling on what such figures are known for, and readings related to their specialties, such as leadership for apostles, sufferings for women and martyrs, study for doctors of the church. For example, for confessor-saints, the prayers point to their preaching: "Servant of God, teacher and worker of miracles, good shepherd among the people, pray for us to the Lord." Courageous martyrs may be invoked to intercede: "Grant by their prayers that we may be freed from the evils that threaten us." Or to serve as models: "May their merits stay with us, Lord, to keep warm our love for you."

At each Office, the cantors open with a phrase or two from a psalm that some monk a thousand years ago decided would be a good way to begin. Chanting, we all answer back, first one side, then the other. The nuns who know what they're doing flip through the colored ribbons. Quick as a frog's tongue catching a gnat from the air, their hands flick from section to section as they chant: red to blue... then to yellow... back to blue... on to green... back to red... then to black.

Once you can change all your ribbons as you are busy chanting, you know right where you are and right where you're headed—in the middle of the life of Jesus, his Mother, the realms of the saints, the foreshadowing of the Hebrews. Once you know how to use them, the ribbons and the chanting pretty much map out the everything of everything.

Ticket to Ride

MISS PITCAIRN, MOUNT ALVERNO'S librarian, is the most nun-like person imaginable who happens not to be a nun. Her short, straight, gray-going-to-white hair crosses her forehead like a window frame, then drops around her ears to the back of her head. She's short enough that I can see right over the top of her head to a carefully tended potted violet and rows of books on the shelves behind her. Usually what she wears matches her hair—gray sweaters, skirts, jackets, jumpers, dresses, shoes, and her once-in-a-blue-moon slacks. Except her blouses, which are almost always white, with little round collars and white buttons and cuffs.

Miss Pitcairn is stand-offish and quiet. You can hardly make out what she says even when she does talk, which isn't often. Things like: "Finding what you need?" Or, "Let's get those magazines out of your way." Of course, in the library no one is supposed to talk except in an emergency. Beyond which, there's the convent Rule of Silence anyway. But I like her. She looks at you with a severe frown, but even then, her blue eyes twinkle.

Miss Pitcairn really helped with my term paper for Sister Ursula's literature class. It was an eye-opener to be introduced by Sister Ursula to

Homer's *Iliad* and Sophocles' tragedies. And weren't they all happening at the same time as the Bible stories I knew from home, the ones I kept encountering in readings for the Office? I wanted to write about whether the Greeks in Homer with their gods—Zeuses and Aphrodites and Mercurys—had any links to the Hebrews with their one God and their Saul and David and Moses and the Burning Bush. And what about the exploits of Gilgamesh in Ancient Babylon? Look at a map and you can see how close everything was to everything else. "There must be connections," I said to myself.

So, for a few weeks Miss Pitcairn let me stack up books and books and more books on the last table of the four at the far end of her library. Every spare moment, I dove into the subject headfirst. Coming from St. Mary's on the prairie up north, I'd never seen so many books in a library before. Our school on Cowlitz Prairie was small—eight kids graduated with me for eighth grade and twenty for high school. Walking to school every day, we crossed the forty-acre field where our cows and horses grazed, talking about the day ahead and looking out at the foothills and snowy mountains. Except for the mountains and the field and the tall trees, nothing was very big.

Our country-school library didn't have a lot in the way of books— mainly a few dictionaries, an encyclopedia, some history books, and quite a few collections of saints' lives. Most of the teachers knew a lot and were smart, so we learned a lot, but our equipment was pretty limited—one or two Bunsen burners to make up a science lab and not much else. I wrote papers the whole time, and we had an encyclopedia and histories of Abraham Lincoln and the American Revolution at home, but I'd never done footnotes the way Sister Ursula wanted, listing every single thing you had read and learned from.

In Miss Pitcairn's library my books started piling up: the tall stack of concordances to every line in the Bible, and next to these a stack of books on the meanings of major Bible stories and figures. Another column almost as tall, on the Greek myths with their various gods and goddesses, and their interpretations. Then, a smaller stack on the gods and stories of other key people in ancient times—Egyptians, Babylonians, Phoenicians, and some you rarely hear of like Medes and Parthians. Right beside stood a short pile of atlases with maps of various empires, of the deserts and the mountains that hindered things and the rivers that connected them, of the trade routes and migrations, and the locations of who conquered and who got conquered, and when.

Within a week, under the weight of all the information headed for my footnotes, the table legs quaked—a lot like the shaking of my own legs at the prospect of it all. But Miss Pitcairn told me it looked about right and gave me cards to write my notes on. These got put into piles too. Calm and steady, she sat behind her desk at the far end of the room as I sank lower and lower behind the stacked-up Ancient World.

My paper made its way from Genesis to Anatolia by way of the Tigris and Euphrates and back again: Patroclus and Achilles against the Trojans, Jonathan and David fighting the Amalekites, Enlil slaying the monster Tiamat, gods and goddesses, heroes and monsters, sacred serpents and evil ones. As sweeping as my paper was, making it all add up to something pretty much eluded me, and my conclusion read less ringingly than I had hoped. But Sister Ursula gave me an "A" for deciding that everybody in the ancient eastern Mediterranean had the idea of a Spirit over Water at the beginning of Everything. Trembling wings of Wisdom with a capital "W" moved the air and foam and the waves beneath.

Now our librarian and I have a chance to get even better acquainted. Sister Agatha has delegated me and Margie—one of my classmates from school on the prairie—to drive Miss Pitcairn home to her retirement center every weekday for the next… well, she hasn't told us yet how long. A terrific assignment after a long silent morning of prayers, work, and classes. I get to venture off our mountain—only the second time since I've been here, and the first hardly counts, since that time we just visited a synagogue in San Mateo with Sister Agatha in charge of everything.

Mount Alverno Convent's Fiat is the funniest looking car ever built. The three of us—Miss Pitcairn, Margie, and me —will hardly fit into it without rubbing elbows and knees as we cram in to drive over to her place at Leisure Meadows in the hills above Woodside. When it's 2:00-ish, time for the trip, I race to the garage and grab the keys from their hook by the door. At the far end of the fleet of Chevies and Dodges and Buicks, like a gray pumpkin on tiptoes, the Fiat perches on its four little tires, ready to sneak away from the convent. Its steering wheel is the smallest I've ever turned. Its square brake- and clutch- pedals belong in a toy car. The slender gear shift curls up out of the floor like a spindly French tulip poised in front of the radio dials, ready to move from gear to gear. On Cowlitz Prairie, it's been strictly American cars and pick-up trucks, so my horizons are expanding.

Exiting the garage, I chug up around the chapel to fetch my passengers. Margie opens the door and pulls the front seat forward so Miss Pitcairn and her flowered satchel can cram into the little backseat. Putt-putt-putt goes the engine as Margie climbs in.

"Oh my!" Miss Pitcairn sighs, once she gets settled, "I do find this little auto worrisome."

"Don't worry," I say in my most reassuring voice, as we turn onto the roadway. "I've been driving since I was eleven years old. We'll get you home just fine."

And we're off. California shines warm and sunny as we wind down our mountain. Palm trees sway over white houses with tiled roofs as we curve down to the business part of things with people in shirtsleeves stopping at service stations or pushing their shopping carts across Safeway parking lots.

Coughing and clearing her throat, Miss Pitcairn calls out above the humming engine. "How in the world did you learn driving so young, my dear?"

"Oh, she grew up in the country," Margie turns and shouts over the motor.

Then I holler out a few bits about haying season back home and my dad teaching me to drive the pickup in our lower field as the Raupp boys threw the hay bales onto the truck to be stacked and hauled off to the barn.

"Once my driving got that far," I yell toward the back with a laugh, "it was no time at all till I was hauling our trash off to the dump."

Snug as a pea-pod, the Fiat hums us down the avenues toward the freeway.

But this *is* quite a change from driving hay to the barn. As we get to the giant highway beside the Bay, a roaring blizzard of traffic whooshes by in lanes and lanes and lanes on all sides. Biting my lip, I turn quiet and attentive to the road as the little Fiat chugs along in the slow lane. Margie turns the radio on and cranks the volume up so we can hear Strauss's "Blue Danube Waltz," one of my favorites. The horns, waltzing in D major, put me in mind of dancing with baby Tim near the record player at home. Ahead, only a couple of exits more, and we'll turn off. We may even still be waltzing.

A gigantic truck roars up behind, its front grill growling in my rearview. I breathe in and out. My right hand turns up the radio then jumps back to the steering wheel. We jiggle our way even slower in the far-right lane. Sure enough, the snarling semi- gives a last thundering growl, swoops around us, and lurches ahead. Whew.... much better! Cars and trucks whizz by on our left as we tootle along. Finally, our exit: "Alameda de las Pulgas"—Spanish for "Poplar Trees with Fleas." That's the kind of thing that makes California great—foreign phrases that are fun to say out loud, and make you laugh when you find out what they actually mean.

As we get off the freeway, the Fiat purrs and climbs as Alameda takes us past more white-with-red tile gas stations, stores, churches and schools, houses, and recreation centers into the sunny hills. Away from the freeway noise, Margie twists around to talk with Miss Pitcairn in the back. I can't think of much to say and actually appreciate the Rule of Silence that's part of being monastic. Sometimes I feel at a loss when it comes to conversation.

Right now, Margie's got it. Clearly happy that we can talk all we like now that we're off the mountain, she jumps in with gusto. How long has Miss P. been at Leisure Meadows? Two years. Mozart or Strauss? She likes Mozart better—more calming. What about the weather? Well, that doesn't get you very far in sunny California.

Margie and Miss Pitcairn discuss California trees as Beethoven now fills our ears. Readjusting the mirror, I see Miss Pitcairn's cap of hair framed by the gleaming cars and sunny ribbon of road behind us. What a top-notch errand for a starting-out, would-be-nun! Past shops, houses, and schools, we wind further into the hills sprinkled with oaks. A deer leaps away from the roadside into the trees. We turn into the parking lot of Leisure Meadows and drive to the far end of Building 2E. Carrying Miss Pitcairn's satchel, Margie walks her to her apartment door. Miss Pitcairn takes the bag, smiles, waves, and turns to the door as Margie dashes back to the Fiat.

My hand jumps to the radio dial. Some quick flips. Zip-zip-zip go the stations. Briskly we spin around the parking lot, exit Leisure Meadows, and head down the hill on our journey back while Bob Dylan's "Like A Rolling Stone" comes over the radio. This reminds me of driving around the prairie running errands for Mom with the music rocking out—then making sure to change the dials safely back from my "communist music" station to one more to her liking that plays Rogers-and-Hammerstein or Brahms.

But here we are now, two Franciscan postulants on the Alameda. Turn up the volume. Crank down the windows. Streaming sunbeams follow as

we curve back down past the churches and neighborhoods and little malls
full of ice cream shops and 7-Elevens. The radio blares. Our black veils
whip about as the car bumps and rattles us down into town.

"How about an ice cream to celebrate?" I holler over the Beatles'
"Ticket to Ride."

Quick as a wink, we spin into an A & W Root Beer stand. A blonde
waitress strolls our way, blinks in surprise as she walks up to us habited
almost-nuns in our dinky car. "Um... Sisters.... May I help you?" she
sputters politely, her left hand pulling at her brown mini-skirt. I don't
suppose she notices that we're all the same age.

"What can we get for less than a dollar?" I ask. It's the total of what I
found in the chapel's lost-and-found drawer, being chapel assistant this
month.

She gulps, hesitates. I help her out. "A soft ice cream cone? Can we
get one of those?"

"Sure," she obliges, "99 cents."

"How about chocolate?" I continue, looking over at Margie.

Agreed.

In no time at all, we're back on Alameda de las Pulgas, sharing an ice
cream.... "To everything / Turn, turn, turn / There is a season / Turn, turn,
turn..." Even the Bible sings out, via the Byrds in harmony.

Pretty soon we're chewing the last of the cone, as the Fiat rattles us
back up to our convent on the mountain. The sun slips below the sweeping foothills to the west, lighting their highest treetops with its last rays.

We enter the wide open iron gates at the entrance. The little Fiat putters
around one more curve to the steep final hill. The sunless amber of early
evening fills the sky. Things start to silhouette against the fading light. As
we make the last climb, the tip of the chapel cross shows at the crest. Then,
up... up... up the mountain we go. More and more of the cross appears:
the top; then its two arms extending; now there it is in its entirety; now

the tile roof of the bell tower that lifts toward the sky. More and more of the tower looms above, till we reach the hill-top and the whole convent is in shadowy view.

We drive around to the garage in back, and once in, find the end spot where the Fiat parks. The bell in the tower rings out for Vespers: *Da-dong, Da-dong.* The first lights twinkle on the hills. We've made it back in time.

The Bells

OUR MOUNTAIN WAKES UP solemnly, high above everybody else's oncoming day. In the canyons coming down from our mountain, suburban streets wind among ranch-style California houses with their lawns and cars and swimming pools and families. Way, way below wakes and bustles a busy layout of freeways, smoking factories, gleaming office buildings, and airports and marinas stretching out along the wide end of San Francisco Bay. But up here, the tall, mission-style bell tower leaps up above the chapel. Red tiles and a cross cap its little roof. A city ordinance says that bells can ring in the day no earlier than six o'clock.

Back home, the Angelus bells sounded from the mission church the same as they do here—three times a day across the prairie. Six a.m. was when Brother Matteo first rang them there too. Then he'd chime them again at noon before lunch and at six p.m. for day's end. The Mount Alverno bells don't need a bell-ringer. A machine pulls at them right on time.

Of course, when the morning bells start here, we've been up for more than an hour already, with meditation, morning prayers, and Office. They sound in that in-between-space that separates the singing of Lauds and the beginning of Mass.

This is when you can stand outside the chapel, lean against the graceful iron railings leading to the giant doors, and look out. If the world is quiet enough and the winds are right, our bells ring out the morning loud enough to shiver the railings, and just behind them you can make out the tiny echoing *plink, plink, plink* of Stanford University's golden tower as it catches the light and rings its bells way down below:

DONG – plink , *DONG* – plink , *DONG* - plink , *DONG* – plink.

No More Idea than the Man-in-the-Moon

1.

EVERY NIGHT WHEN MY dad came home from doctoring in town, we said the rosary, read the Bible and the story of the day's saint, and prayed various supplications for peace in the world, for sick people, for Mary's help with "this vale of tears," and for more people to become priests and nuns to move God and the church forward. Of course, priests and nuns were already part of the family: our cousin Sister Judy in the Midwest, and our beloved monk-uncle, Father Joseph who came to the ranch to visit every Christmas from studying at a university or teaching at the abbey seminary. And Sunday through Saturday, the prayers put it to the next generation: "Bless our family as we bring laborers to your harvest." Mom, Dad, me, and everybody older than the baby recited out loud in a chorus the detailed reminder that young people really need to go to convents and seminaries.

2.

FROM FIRST GRADE ON, the smartest girls at St. Mary's got to the end of senior year and became nuns. Our top baby sitters, Mary Pat and Linda, graduated one May and off they went to the Franciscan convent by fall. The same for my favorite horse-riding friends Barbara and her sister Gloria, who was also my best two-piano-duet partner. Not to mention nearly every one of the valedictorians, scholarship-winners, and May-crowning queens.

Beyond that, when I looked around at the key grown-up people who were women—they were all nuns. Sister Marietta and Sister Martha showed me how to play catch, how to be an ump in baseball, how to stand up for myself. Sister Marie Celine, my brilliant and beloved music teacher, taught me to play piano and organ—Bach, Mozart, and more. By fifth grade, she had me playing the organ for school chapel. By sixth she named me piano accompanist for the high school choir. And by eighth, I won the County Talent Show playing Chopin's *Impromptu* with Sister Marie Celine's beautiful coaching and art.

No doubt about it, it looked like more fun, and more interesting, to be a nun. Most of the nuns laugh a lot more than almost all the mothers and grandmothers I know. Pretty much all the mothers, aunts, and grandmothers I've seen on our Pacific Northwest prairie seemed to get stuck helping their husbands and children look clever and interesting. A lot of them who may have started out smart and talented would end up bedraggled and barely making it through the day.

All the way back to pioneer days, the top girls in a family on the prairie went to the mission school and then joined up. That's how it happened with my first-grade teacher Sister Angela, and also her girl cousins, Sister Epiphania, Sister Noella, and Sister Manuela—who all grew up back home on Cowlitz Prairie. The convent was the obvious river the streams emptied into.

3.

AND THEN THERE WAS Celia.

Our mothers were already best friends when Celia and I were born on the same day in the same Seattle hospital, just before my parents moved to the rural part of the state. In ninth grade, when she came to live at our school on the prairie as a boarder, we started telling each other everything. Maybe she liked boys. During senior year she wrote to her prom date from the year before, whose army draft number had come up. Me, I don't—though I did dance with one now and then, for appearances ... even went to a prom. But Celia's the one I kissed and told everything to.

Then—along with Margie and Monica and Bernadette and a few more of my classmates—she decided to join the convent. I guess at the time that clinched it—even though since being here, she avoids me and we hardly know how to be around each other. Was there a better way than becoming a nun to get off the prairie and turn into a grown-up?

4.

I FOUND HIM FLOATING. His red bucket sunk, underneath the rippling water.

Something in the world stopped.

My dad, the town doctor, couldn't bring him back.

When I turned fifteen, my curly-headed little brother Tommy drowned. The family went into shock. During that fall my parents prayed and yelled and drank more and smiled less. The little kids acted up in school, hanging out with troublemaker classmates and getting reprimanded by their teachers. I couldn't concentrate in my classes and had nothing to say to anyone. All I could think of to do was play the piano.

Tommy was a year-and-a-half when he died. Even though something wasn't right about his legs, he stumbled along all over his world like a little engine with a flat tire, looking for every chance to point and laugh and holler his two words: "bird" and "flower."

On that scorching September day of the funeral Mass in the church, the ceiling fan wobbled around over the congregation, turned on for the only time I can remember. Organ notes from the loft sounded terrible. How could the sun be shining? Sticking to the hot wood of the pew, I hated my dressed-up clothes, my hat, and everything. Father Fabian preached about happy little children being Holy Innocents and going nonstop to heaven to be with angels, and that's why the funeral vestments were cheerful white, and I don't know what else.

Father Fabian had no more idea where Tommy went than the Man-in-the-Moon. I could tell.

In the graveyard, the shovels dropped their sad dirt on Tommy's little coffin.

I decided I had to try to find out what is really going on around here.... go all the way to the horse's mouth. Follow the path of people like Father Joseph and Cousin Judy—people who seem to know.

Marking the Hours

DA-DONG, DA-DONG. When the bells ring, quick, wrap up whatever you're doing at that moment—walking at dawn outside the chapel where the far view stretches to the bay's tidal flats, digging weeds in late morning sunshine in Sister Noella's rose garden, writing a letter home, reading Plato for Philosophy class in the library, saying the Rosary under a eucalyptus, finishing up in the kitchen with the chopped lettuce and celery in the giant salad bowls and the diced tomatoes that will go into supper. Hurry! Get to the first possible stopping point.

Here for a year and received into the order, I'm no longer a postulant in simple black shirt, skirt, and veil. Now I wear the full habit—brown robe with wide sleeves; the narrow outer brown panel of cloth—called the scapular—that hangs front and back from my shoulders over my robe and down to my knees; and the white veil worn by those in the novitiate. After chanting Office every day for a year, I look forward to the Hours shaping the day. Now as a novice, I'll even get my turn as cantor as the year goes on.

Da-Dong, Da-Dong ring the bells again. If you're at work, take off the gingham coverall over your habit, roll down your sleeves, put away your shovel, pen, book, rosary, or knives and board, and head down the long silent corridors to the chapel. Growing up oldest of twelve with my no-nonsense mother, I learned to move quickly from one thing to the next—changing the baby, finishing the dishes, practicing piano, feeding the horses and cows, doing homework. It's the same here: I'm usually one of the first to arrive anywhere.

Low lights glow golden on the oak pews and reflect in the stained-glass windows. The red sanctuary lamp flickers and dances to the right of the altar. The chapel window high above us novices says, "He shall bear thee up, lest thou dash thy foot against a stone." In the quiet, black lace-up shoes tap-tap-tap on the marble, coming in from the two sides of the cloister through openings on either side of the altar—professed sisters in their black veils on the left, striding, or helping others or stooped over their canes. On the right, some postulants whisper, *Shhh!* We novices enter with them and go to our pews in the central nave. A few nuns come in from outside through the giant doors under the organ loft at the back. Everyone goes to her place in the chapel, picks up her breviary, and checks that she's got the pages marked with their correct ribbons for finding her way to each of the Hour's psalms and readings and prayers.

In summer, shafts of daylight from the stained-glass windows throw yellows and reds, browns and greens across the walls and floors at early Lauds and evening Vespers. If it's winter, the candle in the red lamp flickers a jerky, jumping contrast against the dark at those hours. Encased in night, the chapel encircles the flame. The dim space is a still pond with its brown-habited fish swimming to our places for the Hour's chanting.

Right now, the late summer daylight of Vespers threads its way across the shiny floor. My breviary is on its shelf, its pages set, with the red, blue, yellow, green, and black ribbons that I'll turn as we go back and forth between the psalms we sing every time, and the parts just for today and this hour. Sister Agatha raps her knuckles twice, severely, on her pew at the back. We all stand.

Sisters Elena and Kathy, this week's cantors, intone the antiphon from behind, leading the alternating sides. Their voices drift high above, birds on a breeze. Opening bits of the psalm float over our heads, giving the single pitch and the rhythm for our answering verses. Then we all launch into the psalm, one set of chanters intoning, and the other answering.

Over there, they chant:

> *Like the deer that yearns for running streams,*
> *So my soul is thirsting for you, my Lord.*

Here, we respond:

> *Deep is calling on deep, in the roar of waters.*
> *When can I enter and see the face of God?*

Gathering into a tide, the rocking sounds wash back and forth from one side of the chapel to the other in the flickering light.

As our side takes up the verse, every voice measures the words. Slow, even dance steps. The psalm unrolls, word by word, on that one calm, steady note. Now the other side of the aisle answers our verse with theirs. In another forever, we reply as the psalm lifts its way around up to the vaulting roof. Back and forth and back. Each chant makes its way toward the roof and beyond, toward whatever is there.

On big feasts, the Office is lavish with especially beautiful psalms, and instead of singing in today's spare *a capella* manner, we chant along with Sister Mechtilde's organ as it sounds in a smooth wash of chords that surround us. The shifting chords sharing the chant-note transform from one to the next and next and next, as the chanting moves lavishly across a sound-weave, birds floating across a luminous movement of clouds.

On any day, even the simplest, chanting orders the structure of time, carries you along from event to event. Problems and worries—my likely grades in Philosophy class from Sister Mary Barbara; anxiety and loneliness on top of this dry California mountain; how to stay under the frowning radar of Sister Agatha; how to stop hearing the crow's hollow caw-cawing in the cedar over Tommy's casket—any trouble shrinks as the chanting surrounds us.

At any given hour, you can find your place in the realm of the holy ones and the foreshadowing Hebrew history. Chanting the Hours keeps you moving through today in the mysterious center of the universe.

Pulling Out Some Stops

TIME AFTER TIME SISTER Mechtilde interrupted our piano lessons.

"SisTer! ConTaiN. YourSelF. ThaT. PhraSe. aGaiN. WiTh. ReSTrainT. iF. you. PleaSe."

Any drive and flourish in my fingers, arms, shoulders, or even my feet on the pedals required taming. Her rigid counting turned even the swooshing triple-time of waltzes into a (weirdly) mechanical limp. Overall, she managed to make everything smaller and more tedious.

After each lesson, I fled to pound out sonatas and inventions in the deserted parlor or the basement rec room. The piano is a percussion instrument, my fingers reminded me as they sent the padded little hammers inside the piano drumming against their strings. Through the years of lessons on the prairie, my beloved Sister Marie Celine squared my shoulders in third grade to help me sit up tall; listened with me to Mozart on a record the following year, with a quartet score on my lap, as I watched her slender finger move across the score, paralleling the notes of each instrument; and followed me onto the big stage the last year she was at our school, to accept my first-place trophy with me after I blazed through the Chopin impromptu and won the Kiwanis talent show. As my chords banged faster and louder and made that convent piano jump to life, tears stung my eyes.

Okay. Maybe the best way to survive Sister Mechtilde would be to say good-bye to piano-progress and play on my own time, without lessons. Instead, I could study organ with her, which is the only way to have access to the chapel's big electric instrument. The organ's a better fit to Sister Mechtilde's mechanical stuffiness. When I played for chapel and church back on the prairie, the organ, with its on-and-off switch, lined-up foot pedals and keyboards, rows of knobs and levers, and smooth-as-a-flat-roof sound, seemed more machine-like than the piano.

In the high loft near the roof of the cavernous chapel, Mount Alverno's organ gets sunlight twice a day, through stained-glass windows that say, "God sends angels to bear thee up" in glowing letters. This fancy instrument is bigger than anything on the prairie—two wide keyboard manuals and a long set of wooden pedals under the bench, for playing bass notes with your feet. Above the manuals are two rows of round stops to pull out as you play, each labeled for its sound: trumpet, cornet, clarinet, diapason, flute, bass, and so on. To the side, switches of different colors make shimmering tremolos, arching echoes, and other special effects.

Goal for organ lessons: get feet really moving over the bass notes and hands switching back and forth with ease between the keyboards, pulling out stops on the special effects as smoothly as if it's not happening. Especially, learn how to create the backgrounds that Sister Mechtilde improvises to accompany the chanting of the liturgy on Sundays and important feasts. Keep the determined bass notes she's good at, but swell out and spice up her timid chords. Some of those special-effect tremolos and elegant high octaves could lift the chanted psalms for first-class Vespers, Compline, and Lauds like boats on sparkling waves to fill the whole chapel. How about I learn how to play like that and get assigned as organist for some Masses and Divine Office chanting?

Hear This Prayer

O God on the earth: *Graciously hear my prayer.*
O God of everywhere: *Hear me now.*

1.
From Sister Agatha flicking the overhead light
and screaming "Lumen Christi" at the freezing crack of dawn

O Lord, deliver us.

From struggling to get out of bed and habited on time
And stumbling our way to chapel down the cold dark halls

O Lord, deliver us.

From cantors who can't sing leading our chanting
through the Hours of the day all week long

O Lord, deliver us.

From Sister Mechtilde's sniffing
and her prissy music lessons

                              O Lord, deliver us.

From never going anywhere except in a nun-herd
that gets stared at by everyone

                              O Lord, deliver us.

From tip-toeing around Sister Agatha's rules
and wondering half the time what in fact they are

                              O Lord, deliver us.

2.

From the weekly Chapter of Faults and having to think up bad behaviors
that are bad enough to confess but not too bad

                              O God, make haste to help us.

From the sometimes creepy heaviness of
the Rule of Grand Silence

                              O God, make haste to help us.

From getting tired of living on this hot mountain top
with its noisy cities and highways below

                              O God, make haste to help us.

From missing the horses and cows and dogs and cats and rabbits on the ranch
and the forests and all the kids and Mom and Dad

                              O God, make haste to help us.

From that sinking, stone-in-the-water plunk—
"Do I really have a vocation for this?"

O God, make haste to help us.

3.

All ye battalions of angels and archangels
orders of blessed spirits
virgins and widows
monks and hermits
saints and holy people
and all good creatures of the world
graciously intercede and come to our aid.

4.

For singing the Divine Office several times a day,
and bowing and chanting for all the mealtime table prayers

Thanks be to God.

For the beautifully swooshing floor polishers as they gleam up the corridors
with overlapping circles of shine

Thanks be to God.

For the library where Miss Pitcairn lets me stack
all the books I want on the corner table

Thanks be to God.

For the gap through the broken fence to the winding, gnarly trees
at the top edge of the golf course

Thanks be to God.

For the job of sacristan, custodian of a bag of delicious unconsecrated hosts—
a giant bag, way more than we'll ever need for communion

Thanks be to God.

For the butterflies that flutter over the rock roses
at the edge of the cliff

Thanks be to God.

For the sparrows and starlings flying about the bell tower
when the bells ring

Thanks be to God.

For the hawks flying about the mountain
and all the mice and rabbits and lizards that are nowhere to be seen
when they're circling

Thanks be to God.

For my granny shoes that feel as sturdy as cowboy boots
to walk around in and get things done

Thanks be to God.

For the soft scapular of my Sunday habit whipping around
like wings in almost any breeze

Thanks be to God.

For the silence when no one's expected to converse with anyone—
and it's fine

Thanks be to God.

For my guitar and banjo that I can pick and strum if
I finish my duties and studies before Vespers

Thanks be to God.

For the lovely rhythms of each ordered day—even if
I feel a pinch now and again

Thanks be to God.

For a little guidance in figuring out how
to help myself make this work

Thanks be to God.
Amen.

Mixer

FROM SALINAS VALLEY FARM fields, winding into the woods and then—up and up—through one scrubby canyon after another, the two-lane finally takes us to the ridgetop. Narrowing, the road skims farther and farther southward. As evening comes on, moist clouds swallow the last hints of daylight in a thickness you can almost taste. Mists drape the velvety green meadows and the pyramid peaks, which jut above the woods that scatter downward between this high road and the sea. This wet air suits me more than the dusty dry of the South Bay, where the convent perches on its clifftop.

A couple of hours into the journey, an ashen-faced Susan whispered, "Feeling kind of carsick." She wasn't the only one. The jolting of the twisty climb has just straightened out—to the relief of our stomachs.

Even on the gentler ridge, the green Chevy with its sagging shock-absorbers jostles our jammed-into-the-van brigade. Where the heck are we going? Conversation pretty much stopped somewhere down below, as far back as the straightaway near Salinas before the canyons. For a while, the

radio played fuzzy bits of "Like A Rolling Stone" and "R-E-S-P-E-C-T."
Then there was only static, and Father Dominic turned it off.

This trek into the clouds is a first. Until now, we had nothing more
exotic than one-Sunday-a-month guitar Masses in the juvenile hall for
South Bay kids in trouble and locked up. But today we're on our way to
some remote prison camp up in the mountains. Father Dom drives. In
their black shirts and white clerical collars, he and the two seminarians sit
in front, and we eight novice nuns in white veils and brown habits sway
and jiggle in the van's two bench seats in the back.

The sun slips into the roiling fog to the west, after miles and miles
of not a single dwelling or even a fence. In the twilight, we finally take a
right and jounce through the work-camp gates onto a rutted gravel drive
that brings us into a dense forest. A short way in, under the trees, stand
several forlorn barracks that have dropped strips of peeling paint onto
the gravel pathways.

"Okay, good Christians all!" Father Dom hollers, shifting the gears
into park and turning the key. "We've made the trip! Everybody out."

We scramble through the sliding door of the van and down to the
gravel. Immediately, the air dampens veils, habit-sleeves, songbooks,
everything. From beyond the ramshackle one-story buildings comes the
delicious smell of evergreens. The seminarians unload the guitars stashed
behind the back seat. Father Dominic locks up the van and, a large suitcase
swinging at his side, strides toward a lit-up door. We aspiring nuns and
accomplice seminarians shuffle after him across crunching gravel and into
the tin-roofed cafeteria.

A burly prison officer waves from across the room. Advancing between
rows of formica tables, "Sergeant Ernie" (his name tag says) reaches us
clustered at the doorway and gives a gap-toothed grin. "Thank you! Thank
you!" He nods, shaking Father Dom's hand. "It does the boys such a
world of good to have you bring Mass all the way up here to our woods."

Still holding his suitcase in one hand, Father Dom smiles and gives a 'thumbs-up' with the other.

We all set into getting ready for our Mass. The seminarians Ricardo, Dan, and I, the guitar contingent, stroll around the dingy, fluorescent-lit cafeteria with Father Dom, picturing together where to place the altar and our singing spot to best advantage. "How about at that corner?" Ricardo proposes. "Under the brightest lightbulb."

"The guitars can be to one side, with the choir along the other wall … that traps the boys in between," Dan chimes in with a smile. "They'll have to join in whether they want to or not."

"Surround-sound," Father Dom chuckles as he tugs one of the tinny tables to the front. "Here's our altar." Unpacking his Mass-kit suitcase, Father spreads a white cloth on the newly appointed altar and places the chalice, the paten—the special plate for the host—the cruets for pouring the wine and water, the book, and the vestments on a table next to it. As we put together this makeshift church, I'm reminded of back home when we kids played Mass in our family with the handmade Mass-kit that Uncle Cliff and Aunt Irene sent us one year for Christmas. With our smashed Wonder Bread for hosts and Welch's grape juice, we could spend hours in the basement through a rainy afternoon, taking turns playing the parts—priest, altar boys, and parishioners.

"Okay," Father Dom brings me back to California and the prison camp, "let's get these dining tables to the wall and move the chairs into a semi-circle."

Just as the scraping of moving tables and chairs starts, Sergeant Ernie runs to the entrance, blows a whistle, and hollers out the doorway: "Cafeteria-set-up-troop! Get yourselves in here NOW. We've got a church to pull together!"

Within minutes, a delegation of scruffy boys in gray shirts enters, only to huddle near the door. Except for a couple of blue-uniformed guards who come with the boys and stand at the edge of the room, the arrivals are all young—teens and early twenties. Sergeant Ernie marches to the middle of the room, walks around in a circle, gives his whistle a couple of toots, points to the gaggle of inmates, and motions with a tattooed arm: "Inside—inside—inside, you guys!" he hollers. "Get amongst these fine young nuns and priests and move these chairs and tables to where they gotta be."

A youthful meandering follows. Under the dangling lightbulbs in our respective uniforms, bashful young lawbreakers and anxious clericals face each other. "So. Um-m-m-m. Where do you want this stuff?" yells Ernie.

Father Dom takes charge, and in minutes, a hectic banging of furniture transforms the cafeteria. Gray-shirted toughs join the habited nuns, shoving all tables except the designated altar and the one for the Mass prep up against the wall.

"Sister, would you like some help with that table?" a lanky Latino boy asks Susan quietly. "My name is César." Smiling, she nods.

We guitar players place three folding chairs on one side of the altar beside a rolling-cart for our music stand. Seven chairs for the choir of novices are arranged in two rows on the other side. In a semicircle in between, Sister Kathy and a blonde-mustachioed inmate calmly space several dozen chairs in even semi-circular rows for the prison congregation. Father Dom places the candles, chalice, book, and cruets on the altar, then begins donning his vestments. The novices now hand out mimeographed sheets and urge the inmates to move toward chairs.

"Here you go—the songs and prayers that you'll need." Sister Bridget offers papers to one bashful boy, then another, then another. Smiling, she grabs the first tall inmate by the arm and hauls him to the front row: "You guys really want to sit here so you can hear better and catch on to the singing." Three or four shuffling boys follow Bridget and her tall friend, taking their sheets, smiling awkwardly, and reluctantly following her congregational advice.

Amidst the getting-ready bustle around us, Ricardo, Dan, and I place our chord sheets on the serving-cart, pull guitars from their cases, and start to tune. Leaning over my trusty Gibson, I turn my tuning peg to match my E string to Dan's resounding E. Something thoughtful, still, and calm settles over this jumpy moment of hasty, yet detailed, listening and preparation.

In the past couple of months, the four times we played other prison Masses, I was a nervous wreck—me, the younger Franciscan-convent girl trying to keep up with the older, quick-fingered seminary guys. Back on our family ranch, I learned guitar by matching chords to popular radio hits and trying familiar sing-along songs. But in those detention-hall Mass situations, the slightly show-off seminarians were usually too busy bossing everyone around to take time to practice. Once the service started, my fingers raced and fumbled to keep up as their hands jumped like rabbits from chord to chord. Their playing gave me a lot to aim for. Already in their manly mid-twenties, they often smiled indulgently in my direction.

"Make me a channel of your peace"—D chord, B minor... strum-strum-strum... quick jump to A... then A7. I did my best to follow Dan's barred versions at his guitar's fifth fret, sometimes totally faking it. Maybe just to throw me off, one of them sometimes dropped out altogether while the other doodled some fancy notes up the neck. Je-e-e-e-sh! They strutted about in their newly-donned clerical collars and always played too loud—which was good for covering my off-notes. But it *was* fun. Sometimes Ricardo and Dan went out of their way to help me: "Here, when you play a G chord, try hammering-on to the B string to punch it out, syncopated." Or, "Make your bass line ascend up the scale while we follow with high chords on the off-beats."

I got used to listening, watching, grinning back at them with a little nunny-smile as my fingers found chords and strums that had never occurred to me before. By now, way out here in some watery far-off woods, my guitaring is starting to seem just about right.

When things are ready for our Mass, a factory whistle shrieks, and a fuzzy-faced redhead named Billy goes to the open cafeteria door, ringing a hand bell. The furniture-movers take seats in twos and threes behind Bridget's front-row cohort, while more boy-men jostle through the door and slouch into the remaining folding chairs. Beyond our formica altar, above the mostly shaven heads, nubbly beards, and work shirts, stand concrete sinks, ancient dishwashing machines and hoses, and behind them ramshackle stoves and ovens. Somber guards usher the newcomers into the room, then space themselves against the walls in some planned, guarding way. In this forest camp, elaborate prison rules and stern enforcement curiously mix right alongside something helter-skelter and drifty—kind of like the convent.

With the altar candles lit and everyone in place, Father Dom gives the nod, and we guitar-players strike up.

"People of God, come on in, come on in, come in, / People of God, come on in, come to the Table of the Lord." The novices stand sprightly and sing on cue. The inmates rise unevenly into slouchy stances. The first time through, the "people of God" are pretty feeble—nuns and guitar-players randomly shadowed by an intermittent and reluctant grumble of male voices.

Then, taking charge of the situation, Ricardo breaks guitar-player ranks, leaps toward the bashful and sullen prisoners, and jumps up and down, his guitar around his neck and his black hair flopping over his forehead. "Vengan, boys! *Vengan!*" His shrieks echo to the tables bunched at the far end of the room. "Come on, you people! Come on!" he shrieks, "We keep at it till YOU SING LOUD!!!!"

Back to the top: "People of God, come on in" ... It takes only two repeats with Ricardo dancing around and shouting like a crazy-man for the boys to get over their sulkiness. By verse three, the whole cafeteria—except for the guards, who are probably paid to stay sulky—echoes and jumps and sways. Guitars and voices peal to the rafters under the tin roof, pans rattle with joyful harmony over the stove at the far end.

Our New Franciscan

DAWN EDGES THE PEAKS at the end of the bay. The morning star twinkles. Soon more and more light will creep up behind to pull the day across in the east. After a while, inside the chapel the risen sunbeams will drive through the stained-glass window behind the professed sisters, streaming across the tile floor in front of the altar to give the morning Mass a fiery glow.

We've all been up for hours by now, what with Sister Agatha the novice mistress hollering "Lumen Christi" up and down the dark halls at 4:30 a.m. Wake up. Dress silently: brown under-habit, lighter brown scapula, white novice veil, black knee socks, black tie-up shoes. Then it's on to chapel for meditation before we chant the morning Office.

As always, I only need five minutes to get habited, so there's plenty of dawn-time for my long walk through the eucalyptus trees to watch the daylight creep up. Birds rustle in the trees and along the ground at the cliffs on the eastern edge of the mountain. City lights and ribbons of freeway still twinkle across the basin below. After a while I head back to chapel and my place for meditation and Lauds and Mass. By the time all that's done, the birds are busy at their day, chattering away in the bell tower. As we process in two silent rows down the hallway from morning chapel for breakfast, I can tell, today is going to be another beauty.

We novices reach the turn to the refectory. Sister Monica, Superior of the House, stands way down the hall, looks me straight in the eye, and points directly at me. As crisp and business-like as a person can be, at this moment she frowns her eyebrows more than usual and motions with her hand for me to break out of the line going in to breakfast. A scientist with a lab full of malaria mosquitoes, she experiments on them for the government. Assigned to the lab as a postulant for my very first work post, I had to feed the mosquitoes on white mice every day: syringe the furry things temporarily to sleep, lay them out in their dreamland on the netted top of a glass box full of mosquitoes, and watch the buzzers swarm up to the net to lunch on the little sleeping rodents. By far, the most disturbing job so far. When my three-month stint ended, my heart lifted; as assistant-chapel-sacristan it was simply dusting and polishing; folding and unfolding vestments, and setting things out for liturgies. (A high point of that post, besides not having to anesthetize mice: the arrival of a carton of new, as yet unconsecrated hosts for Mass that I made sure to taste-test as I put them into their storage containers in the sacristy. The papery little circles, especially munched in two's and three's, have a musky-sweet cracker-y taste.)

Why is Sister Monica beckoning me even before breakfast? Looks like I'll be talking, long before lunch when it's allowed, without having to sneak in a conversation. Definitely necessary if the Superior of the House says so.

"Listen," she whispers as I approach, with my hands folded, nun-like, inside my wide brown sleeves. "A newborn fawn is in the bushes under the flagpole in front of the chapel. The doe ran off. I'd like you to see what you can do."

Sister Monica taught on the prairie at my school when I was young and knows I grew up ranching with calves and colts and lambs.

"Maybe mother will come back if we stay clear of her fawn," I say.

"Not likely," Sister Monica replies. "She ran off when I came out to raise the flag. By now, cars will be coming and going in the parking lot all the rest of the day."

Finding an old cotton blanket in a linen closet, we hurry down the polished hallway to the front door and outside to the flagpole. Maybe it's gone? No, there it is, a tiny, gooey, curled-up pile of bones. My mind flashes back to the twin lambs my mother fed in the kitchen when I was six. Worse, the early morning throat-rattle of the cocoa-colored foal—so carefully tended those three days when I was fifteen—until he died in my lap. Oh dear.

Sister Monica has no idea what to do. But I guess I have a few. "Where can I be with the fawn? We'll need a heater, a dim light, and more blankets."

The stars and stripes *flap-flap-flaps* on the flagpole above us as I open the white blanket, tuck it around the shivering fawn, and take into my arms the shivering weight of a tiny calf, or of a very early-born foal. I slowly place a soft flap of the blanket over its eyes—probably better if the slimy little bundle doesn't even *try* to figure out what's going on. The three of us head back inside the convent and downstairs to a basement storeroom at the end of a long dark hallway I've never been to. A black desk lamp gets plugged in and an electric heater warms up a crowded storage room. Worn sheets and blankets fill a box, and I nestle the fawn down in its bed. What next?

It has to learn how to eat, or it will die like the colt. I can't bear the thought of that again. Sister Bernie brings a couple of baby bottles from Sister Wilma's charity supplies for mothers and their new babies. The fawn looks up from the box, almost buried in a mound of blankets. The heater hums on a stack of boxes, where I hope it will stay put. I head for the kitchen to try to concoct something like deer milk.

I remember trying to bottle-feed Sheba's colt when it wouldn't nurse. Okay. Babies like things sweet. That was as true with my little brothers and sisters as it was with the lambs and foals. Add some Karo corn syrup for sweetening to a pan of milk heating on the stove. Stir it in. Then a little water to thin down the cow's milk so it's more like everybody else's. Warm it all up. Pour it into the bottle. Here's hoping the fawn gets the idea. My heart jumps. I wonder if St. Francis has us under watch right now.

Back below, I open the heavy storage room door. The lamp next to the whirring heater throws a soft light. I step in. Hope the little bundle still quivers. Sitting cross-legged next to the heap of blankets, I make sure my brown habit stays under my gingham-coverall apron. No telling where this hopefully-like-deer's-milk will end up. Placing the warm bottle next to me on the floor, I gently pull the still-breathing fawn onto my lap. Poor thing. Being new to life is strange enough without finding yourself with a nun instead of your mother. Well... here goes.

My right hand takes the bottle as my left cradles the still-gooey little face. My index finger presses near the fawn's mouth, rubs softly, coaxes it to think about sucking. At first, nothing. Then the quivery little mouth wakes up... gets interested... wraps around the finger.... tries to get going. Quickly my hand tips the warm bottle over and nestles its milky nipple next to my finger. "That's it. You've got the idea. Take a-hold, little guy. You can do it."

At first halting, clumsy, puzzling, the two of us bumble about in the messy storage closet with this mama-nun baby-deer arrangement. But soon, the hungry little fawn figures it out. Opens one eye. Looks at me. Drinks down most of the bottle. I'm still holding my breath, but things look good.

For the next day or so, I'm on edge. Keep remembering the motionless cocoa-colored foal on my lap in the shed at the edge of the barn—his little throat rattling that he was gone. Fuss and re-fuss over my deer-milk formula. By day two, my fellow-novice-pal Sister Margie joins me on basement fawn duty. We take turns making up and warming the deer-milk and doing the feedings, keeping the fawn company, and cleaning our fawn-and-its-novices-quarters. We're pretty much relieved of our usual duties—prayer-life, work in the kitchen, theology classes, Rule of Silence. After all, Sister Monica is Superior of the House, and we are a Franciscan Order. This kind of thing takes precedent.

After a few days, Margie and I are desperate for sleep. But the fawn is definitely making it in the world. Lively as anything, she hears us at the door, jumps right up, and runs for her bottle. We decide to call her "Joy." Well, that's Margie's suggestion. Truth be told, it's a bit optimistic for my taste. I'd prefer something edgier. But I can't think of anything to suggest. In no time at all she trots across the closet to us the minute we say "Joy." I take to kissing the top of her head. Before long, she'll be strolling in the outdoors like a proper deer.

I wonder if she'll think of herself as a Franciscan?

Things of a Child

I am become like a pelican in the wilderness,
like a night raven in the house.
I have watched and am a sparrow all alone on the housetop.

(PSALM 101:7-8)

Back at the mission graveyard, beside the small grave,
old Father Fabian, for all his talk of angels,
had no idea where that kid went ...
                    or the little colt.

        I came to Mount Alverno
                    for answers.

And ...
all this theology
        and philosophy
                and meditation

           and prayer

                 and contemplation later,

I don't know, either.

It's just the crunch of the dirt on the little coffin,
and a single crow rustling the cedar,
and hollow shells strewn on the beach by the tide,
and the keening of the mare for her foal,
and the blood left behind,
            and how to live with it.

When I was a child, I spoke as a child, I felt as a child,
I thought as a child.

                  (1 CORINTHIANS 13:11)

Now,

         ... a sparrow
      all alone on the housetop.

Drunken Swallows

IT'S THAT TIME OF YEAR. The swallows who live in the bell tower get tipsy on the overripe crimson berries on the bushes below. They cluster all over the branches, then fly up to the tower and hurl themselves down helter-skelter off the top, chirping and chattering and carrying on with an amazing racket.

Yesterday, one got into the chapel, nobody knows how. In a panicked state, it flew around all through Vespers and beyond, disturbing the silence afterward as it desperately tried to find a way out through the stained-glass window near the vaulted ceiling. By the time we came back in the dark for Compline, the chapel was quiet. Did it get out?

Now at the edge of the cliff, dawn comes on over the Bay, and the spicy smell of eucalyptus lifts with the mist. How long have I been at Mount Alverno? Is this all a confusing mistake? My best-loved horse, Sheba, has died back on the ranch. They haven't even told me how. My dad often sends me little notes on his prescription pads, usually a sentence or two. That's all I hear about things at home. And I miss the prairie and the big woods. Everything here is so up above everything else and yet hemmed in. Here I am, committed to another day of Lauds, and Grand Silence, and studying the Trinity, and waxing and polishing Sister Delphine's endless corridors. Down below, the whole busy world hums with freeways and factories and buses and universities. Coming here was the only way I knew to get off the prairie—now, getting off this mountain is even harder to picture.

At moments, this cocoon of devotions and study feels good. But I'm not any closer to knowing where baby Tommy went after he died. I feel at ease in a fleeting session of singing with my guitar, or playing the organ for Mass, or breathing in a relieving draught of cigarette smoke up in my secret place on the roof, in the middle of the night, the moon spotlighting the silent convent. Sometimes I've been tickled to share a secretive nip of whiskey with Sister Marietta in the kitchen pantry. She gets me my cigarettes. Don't ask me how. She's been an inspiration going all the way back to first grade on the prairie when I followed her around as she polished the school's long corridors, or hammered nails, or swept the leaves off porches. It's fun to joke with her, smoke Marlboros, and drink Jack Daniels now that I'm grown up and a nun to boot.

But I've got to sort things out. *Da-dong. Da-dong.* The bell rings Lauds.

I turn, trudge up the hill from the mountain's edge, make my way to chapel. Sure enough, with daylight coming on, the drunken birds are full-tilt with their wacky chirping and careening.

God's Knitting Needle

NOW, AS THE NEW SCHOOL TERM APPROACHES, we first-year novices receive dire warnings from the second-years about Father Aegidius, who'll be teaching our required liturgy class. "Just don't let him scare you," they whisper, looking as wide-eyed and rattled as if they were talking about a ghost. They've already made it through the completely cloistered year that I'm cloistered in now. On the other side, they're free to think about a few things besides God.

Last year, as brand-new postulants, we took classes at the convent in English, psychology, biology, and philosophy, attended a special Current Events weekend class on the Civil Rights Movement, and even went to Stanford University to hear Father Daniel Berrigan speak against the war in Vietnam. Such up-to-date, worldly activities can't happen now that we're in our year of contemplative super-cloister. As a beginning novice—canonicals, we're called—along with wearing my new, regular Franciscan habit, I must focus only on spiritual topics. Eventually each of us will study to work as a teacher or a nurse or a counselor. None of that now. All through the year it's nothing but silence, prayer, contemplation, theology, scripture, and wearing gingham for a good part of each day as we silently work hard around the Motherhouse.

On the first day of liturgy class with Father Aegidius, I choose a seat in the front row near the door. We're around the corner from the convent chapel and down the hall from Sister Monica's science lab. With the warnings from the second-years, we canonicals scurry to the room early and perch on the edge of our seats, waiting for the notorious professor. Seconds *tick-tick-tick* around the clock above the door. Somebody sneezes... drops a pencil... picks it up.

A few minutes after the hour—*ka-lomp, ka-lomp, ka-lomp, KA-LOMP*—down the hall. The door flares, bangs wide against its stopper, and in strides a figure in black cape and cowl. One hand swings a worn leather briefcase, the other a rumpled black umbrella. *THUD*—the briefcase drops to the table. The umbrella handle hooks over the chair at the front of the room. His back to us, the gigantic Father Aegidius unclasps and swirls the black cape of his Benedictine habit, turns, then flops its dark folds over the umbrella. His hands flip back his hood, tug at the black skirts cinched by his leather belt, then slick back long strands of thinning hair from his forehead. Straightening and clearing his throat, he addresses us with some kind of foreign accent:

"Goodt Morningk," he declares. I crouch as far back in my seat as possible. My thick black stockings itch as my calves press hard against the frame of my desk. I feel my eyes widen in their sockets. No matter how prepared you thought you were, it's hard to feel at ease in *this* liturgy class.

Father Aegidius stalks from one end of the classroom to the other announcing: "Vee are here to shtudy the Theyology und Prakteece of Catholic lee-turgy." Father Aegidius, on closer inspection, is not very old. Despite his balding pate, the hairs that periodically flop onto his forehead and then get smoothed over are black, not gray. And he's agile as a cat. Pacing around the front of the room, he turns with dips and spins, pauses, looks to the ceiling, pokes the air with a finger as he talks. Wire-rimmed glasses, as thick as bottles, cover his darting black eyes. When he peers my way through the magnifying lenses, his left eye gazes in one direction, and the right goes off in another. His words don't always come across, and not only because of his moving and darting around, or even the accent. His two front teeth are spaced so far apart from each other that one might be missing. His tongue snarls up in the words as he speaks.

Before the class I never gave a thought to "Mosaic Law transformed into Pauline teachings," or "the theology of transubstantiation and the real presence in the eucharistic sacrament." Oh dear! I would venture a question, if I thought I could make sense of the answer.

Finding myself scared to death of the guy, I'm turning up as much information on Father Aegidius as possible. I guess it was Sister Agatha—newly promoted to being in charge of the novitiate—who told us during the summer that a monk from the Benedictine Priory in the hills above Woodside would drive here to Mount Alverno to teach us liturgy. She said he was from somewhere in Eastern Europe—a refugee who escaped; she thought maybe during the Czech uprising against the Russians. My family was always big on stories about Catholics who came from behind the Iron Curtain, sneaking out at night over the borders and leaving everything behind. A Hungarian family came to our prairie church when I was young, then moved on to Seattle. Anna, my mother's best friend in our parish at home, escaped from Latvia just a few years ago.

At mealtimes in the refectory, when talking is allowed, I ask around about Father Aegidius. Bits and pieces come from the older novices. Sister Leticia also speculates that he's Czech, from a monastery over there, and only learned his English here, and recently. Or, "maybe from Transylvania," says some smarty, as the whole table snickers. Last week at supper, someone said she'd heard he escaped from a Communist prison and somehow got to the Benedictine monastery here in California after that. Sister Mary Matthew says he's got to be older than he looks… that he survived torture over there by the Nazis as a young monk, only to get into trouble with the Russians a few years later. Everybody agrees on one thing: Father Aegidius has a rough and desperate history.

With the term halfway through, my grades can't be going well, given that Father Aegidius objects to my every answer when he calls on me. He tells us our exams "vill be very longk and very hardt." These days, I head straight for the back row to stay out of his line of vision. With each lecture, our professor seems more agitated. Pacing the room from one end to the other, he'll shout out a topic—something about the Mass or chanting the Divine Office, about how the performance and devotion by priests and brothers and nuns create the absolute whole meaning of everything. Occasionally he intones Latin in growling bass tones, closing his eyes and keeping time with his bony hands. The windows seem to rattle.

Around midterm time I sit in the chapel at night, doing my best to meditate the way we're supposed to, before Compline. A phantom scene floats into my mind—grainy black-and-white, like a newsreel-still from the movies of World War II times:

A skinny seminarian looks through wire-rimmed glasses. He's no older than I am now. Smokestacks of the terrible ovens loom against a stormy sky. Behind tangles of barbed wire, he stands in a long line of skeletal Jews, Communists, Catholics, and other undesirables.

Our professor takes to chalking furiously on the blackboard: circles within circles within squares within circles within squares. It's baffling, if obviously important to him—like the mysterious interlacing petroglyph cliff-carvings above the Columbia River back home: full of incomprehensible significance. He's telling us something about how the Divine Office works when we chant. In any given class his whole blackboard gets covered with intersecting chalk marks—tangled and retangled and tangled again.

Who can find a way through *this*?

At one point in his lecture, Father Aegideus lurches to the right and draws a quick spiral that turns into a big chalky arrow zapping from the upper right corner. "Zee Eye of Godt!" he exclaims as the chalk slashes its way down across the board. Seeing *everything*, the line cuts through all the circles-within-circles-within-squares, the entire width of our classroom from the upper corner of the board down, down, down, down to the far lower left.

Once "the Eye of God" gets to its destination, I just know someone's going to get pointed at and called on to have the right answers about what God sees in all that chalk. I sit in a sweat, hands shaking, heart pounding.

Back in chapel, once again in a quiet moment between liturgies—Lauds, Mass, Vespers—I puzzle over how chanted prayers apparently have something to do with the cosmos, the universe, and everything else there is. As usual, I worry about liturgy class. What is the scary professor trying to tell us? My mind forms another scene:

Russian soldiers frown under their ear-warming flaps. They're smoking unfiltered cigarettes, stamping in the snow, holding shiny rifles at the ready. A rickety farm truck reaches the checkpoint, chock-full of Slavic

vegetables: purple cabbages; nose-tingling onions; bright orange car-
rots; dirty pink potatoes. The bearded driver brakes with muddy boots.
Loaded gunnysacks, covered over with produce, ride behind him. Inside
the biggest sack, heaped over in one corner of the truck-bed, scrunches
up a younger, gaunt, tight-rolled but still massive Father Aegidius.
Inside the burlap, he holds his breath. Prays not to sneeze. Hopes to
stay cabbage-covered. Remembers whatever trouble he's gotten into
with the Russians. Pretends to be nothing but a desperate bag of pota-
toes trying to get across the border. On his way to what turns out to be
sunny California.

That week, I get a "D" on the midterm exam. That's a first. I don't talk
about it. Sisters Margie and Susan and Bridget didn't do any better.

One day, Father Aegidius stomps into class in the usual way and opens
his tattered leather bag. Instead of notes, or a book, he pulls out a powder-blue ball of yarn. Holds it up for us to see. "Time is a great mee-
sterry," he declares. Unwinding the yarn, he solemnly drops it in swirls,
the draping loops spilling over his sandals. Then he winds it all up back
into a ball in his left hand, holds it out in front of himself, and pulls out
the yarn in its single strand with his right. Slowly he extends both his
arms—the lengthening strand in one hand, moving away from the coiled
ball of yarn in the other—as far apart as his long limbs can reach. Time
as yarn: messy as we live it out on the one hand; rolled up in the calendar
on the other.

"We joost walk along zuh leetle yarn," he says, twirling the single,
straight blue strand between his outstretched hands. "Zat is all we know:

walk, walk, walk." He ambles and circles the front of the room. "But, vhat dost Godt see vhen we chant zee Office?"

His black eyes blink-blink-blink behind his thick glasses. Suddenly he rewinds the single strand of yarn back into the ball as fast as he can. Reaching into his briefcase with that lurch I'm no longer startled by, he pulls out a good-sized knitting needle. Holding the yarn in his left hand, he pounces as he stabs the silver needle into that fluffy, powder-blue ball with his right.

And I get it.

There we are, on God's knitting needle. As if we're sitting astride its silver length, the day's chanting rides us along with "Zee Eye of Godt." That intersecting needle angles us across the winding, balled-up strands of time, which otherwise we only picture pulled out in the skinny little line where we happen to be walking. This morning's chant, in this year's season, intersects a story of Moses always read for this day's feast, with an echo of it in something from Jesus, a plea for help and blessing in the words of Isaiah, a psalm from David calling for peace. Across rolling strands of orbiting time, this season's prayers and chants transect us, just as they did last year. Exactly as they did for singing monks and nuns a hundred years ago... or some thousand... or a few.

And then you have to ask, what do we have at the center? Only the fuzzy beginning of a string at the start of its winding, I guess. But what's around this fuzzy start makes a circling world in the chanting of it, charged with something celestial. Maybe something like God.

Every day from then on, as I did every day before, I chant Lauds before Mass. Now the psalms fit better—anxious and wringing their hands for Advent; shimmering their cymbals on a joyful feast; weeping Lenten tears. Each morning, the Mass carries it all further, orbiting us along our way in the liturgy galaxy.

The term ends. I pass liturgy class with a C+. Another first in my schooling. Christmas comes with its Hours and Masses full of shining psalms, rising suns, and blossoming Rods of Jesse.

When school starts back up in January, there's no liturgy course. The second semester of the class is cancelled. Someone whispers that Father Aegidius suffered a nervous breakdown over the holiday.

I picture the agitated, pacing Father Aegidius with his knitting needle. Think a little prayer. Conjure him in a new posture.

Taking a deep breath, a tall, gaunt Benedictine monk sits on the desk, reaches into the shabby briefcase at his side for a powder blue ball of yarn and puts it in his lap. He takes up the soft, single strand in one hand, a shining needle in the other. His fingers slowly tie the strand to the needle, and then he casts on in the usual way. From the bag he takes the partner needle. Sits on the desk. Smiles. Quietly knits.

Improvisation

IT'S HARD TO IDENTIFY what I've learned from Sister Mechtilde. She supplies me with books, sheet music for hymns, and liturgy settings now that I've given up piano lessons with her and am only studying organ. But she doesn't really teach. When she demonstrates a piece at my lesson, I watch her, especially the darting of her gleaming shoes over the bass pedals. But, tips for how to do it? She hardly has anything to say except: "SisTer. ThaT PhraSe aGaiN, PleaSe. ThiS TiMe, CorrecTly iF You WoulD."

Mostly, I just come away with a bad attitude. I guess I'll have to stay at it for seventy or eighty years until "correctly" just happens when I'm as old as Sister Mechtilde.

I've observed on my own a few ways she gets the chords moving for the Office chants on first-class feast days. Her fingers crawl smoothly over the manual keys with connecting movements, while underneath, her feet on the bass notes shape distinct rhythms and mark the chord shifts with forceful jumps, walking-bass lines, and sometimes dramatic note-changes. When I'm below in the chapel as we all chant the Office, say on the feast of St. Francis, or on a Saturday at First Vespers, I listen closely to her organ-playing above. The next day, I get the psalter with the musical settings of the psalms and turn to those that we chanted, trying to recreate what I remember of her chord changes and especially those strong, lumbering bass notes.

Playing organ for Mass at St. Francis Mission parish, my mom always took her shoes off so her stocking-feet could really feel the bass notes. On a lively hymn like "Holy God, We Praise Thy Name," her toes jumped all over the line of smooth wooden pedals on the little organ. At a key word or chord change, Mom's unshod left foot stomped one of the lowest notes at the far left of the pedal board decisively, giving "Holy God" a satisfying growl.

Without question, Sister Mechtilde would have none of that stocking-foot-playing—if she knew about it. Which, of course, she won't.

I play piano on my own now, when no one's around. Sometimes in the parlor. Sometimes the empty rec room. I keep it random and stealthy, just in case it'd be considered some kind of infraction. On Tuesday mornings when I don't have class, Sister Mechtilde meets me in the chapel loft for my organ lesson. I give *"Tantum Ergo"* and "I Am the Bread of Life" a go, as best I can with my shoes on.

The *real* pay-off comes each day for an hour or so when I find the giant chapel empty and quiet, lit only by the flickering red lamp in the Sanctuary and whatever sunlight filters yellow and pale-green through the stained-glass at the edge of the roof. Far at the back, I climb the winding stairs to the loft, almost up to the sunlit windows. Turn on the small tube-lamp over the keyboards. Open my hymnbooks. Take off my shoes. Flip the "ON" switch, and slide onto the wide wooden bench. My feet slither across the smooth bass pedals as I familiarize my toes with their keyboard, help them picture stepping on their notes, scales, and intervals, in time with my fingers playing on the manual keys.

Awash in a sunbeam if I'm lucky, I begin with the pieces assigned at my last lesson... something short—maybe the "*Sanctus*" that I'm preparing to play for real at an upcoming Mass. First, I go over the bass parts, my toes feeling the pedal-edges from one note to the next. The second time through is simple—getting comfortable with the coordination of my hands and feet. By the third time, my feet know just where to go, as my hands jump back and forth between the two manuals and their contrasting settings. The upper keyboard sounds high and reedy—"Holy, Holy, Holy." Then both hands jump to the doubling notes of the lower keyboard, with a high and low octave—"Lord God of Hosts." At the final measures of "Hosannah in the highest!" the drama heightens as my left foot lands clean on the low bass tonic, while my right finds a harmonizing upper fifth.... Sweet!!! Meanwhile, my left hand holds the chords on the lower manual as my right, quick as a whip, pulls three more stops, then lands high on the upper manual with a chord that shimmers with the glittering effects of high octave, trumpet, and tremolo.

"Hosannah in the highest," for sure.

I turn to improvising chords to accompany the chanting of psalms for a high feast. Sister Mechtilde gave me a book of psalm settings that supplies the key for each and roughly outlines how the words will fall in the chant. But exactly how the chords hover, with notes blending from one to the next and the bass framing it all below, is left to the organist to make up. In the rhythm for chant, as free and flexible as water, the music finds and shapes the unfolding of the words. I doodle around a while with this improvising.

Finally, toward the end of my practice time, as the setting sun leaves the chapel dimmer and dimmer, my fingers whisk from the lower manual to the reedy upper, then back with increasingly adventurous special effects from new combinations of stops. My chords wash with quirky, enjoyable shifts. One of my favorite moves for the bass: below the shimmering chords in G major for Psalm 149, "Sing to the Lord a New Song," my feet start sounding a pronounced

DUM – da DUM... da DUM...
G   G C   C D
da DUM DUM
C   A

Smoothly taking their cue, my chords at the keyboard join the gentle bass ostinato, which anyone with the proper musical background might recognize:

Sloopy li – ives ... in a very ... bad part of town,
And EVERYBODY (yeah) tries to put my Sloopy down ...
      Ha -a -ang on, Sloopy,
      Sloopy, Hang on !
      Ha -a -ang on, Sister,
      Sister, HANG ON !

Amidst the Furnace

In those days the Angel of the Lord went down into the furnace
with the companions and drove the flame of fire out of the furnace,
and made the midst of the furnace like the blowing of a wind
bringing morning dew.

(DANIEL 3:47)

Like an officiating priest facing an altar,
Sister Regina in the laundry invokes "Madre María dulcísima,
    fortísima, potentíssima!" at the top of her voice,
    "Bring to us your blessings NOW."

This blazing laundry
    and its robed companions could sure use
        a breeze blowing in
            some morning dew.

All in a Day's Work

THE LAUNDRY—OH, NO! Nobody wants that assignment, especially in spring and summer when all the turbo washers and dryers and mangles heat the place to a cauldron. Laundry wins the prize for hardest and least popular novitiate job, hands down. It also takes the most time— that and kitchen. Washing clothes and cooking meals for a community of a hundred-and-some women—those are heavy jobs.

For that reason, the Novice Mistress fills those assignments—two for Sister Regina's laundry; two for Sister Wilma's kitchen—from the ranks of the canonicals. As first-year novices, in addition to heaps of contemplation and spirituality, no classes but theology and lessons in devotion and Franciscan rule, hours of extra silence and seclusion, if your chips fall on Laundry or Kitchen, you also get day after day after day of hot, hard work.

I'm almost nineteen, it's unusually hot in late spring, and I am in a steamy racket of grinding gears, sloshing water, and roiling and roaring dryers. Above this din, Sister Regina's voice barks orders and hollers out prayers and litanies as she scurries from roaring machine to roaring machine. Adjusting their dials and levers with one hand, she wipes the perspiration from under her veil with a handkerchief in the other. At the top of her lungs, she launches into breath-taking improvisation.

"Our Blessed Lady of Perpetual Help," her Californio accent catapults over the mechanical thunder, "and Mother of Tender and Boundless and Everlasting Kindness!" She's making this up as fast as her mouth can move, and it sounds something like "How-er Blay-sayd Lay-dee off Pear-pay-chew-all Haylpb." And on like that.

"Pray for us!" Sister Bernie and I scream at the top of our voices, our reply barely audible.

"Our Lady of Eternal Grace and Pity and Smiles and Blessings and Justice!" she continues.

"Pray for us!" we shriek.

"Holy Mother, Protector of All God's Poor and Weak and Hungry and Troubled Children!"… And so it goes.

Finishing its load, the washer buzzes its need to get emptied. Jumping to heed it, I cross the room and unlock its circular steel and glass door. Caught up in the task, I lose track of the litany in the tangled heap of wet clothes. Sashaying behind me, Sister Regina playfully snaps me with a towel of reminder.

"Uh-h-h, yeah," I blurt out. "Pray for us!"

Rhythm restored, on we go through every imaginable Blessed Virgin epithet she can concoct. From there we proceed to our needs for deliverance: "From Pestilence, Famine, War, Starvation, Sickness, and Every Misfortune!"

"Deliver us, Oh Lord," Bernie and I cry out as we load and unload, fold, stack, and shelve. From disasters and sickness, we move on to ask for curative, clarifying, and general buck-up prayers from as many saints and their trademarks as come to mind.

"Holy Father St. Francis, Tamer of the Fearsome Wolf and Sweet Protector of God's Little Birds!"

"Pray for us!"

St. Teresa the Great with her great thoughts, her feather pen and book; Theresa the Little Flower with her pink and yellow roses and the gift of humility; the brave St. Sebastian and his chest full of arrows; apostolic St. Peter, upside-down on his cross in Rome; steadfast St. Lawrence, calmly sizzling on the griddle; the musical St. Cecilia playing the organ next to the martyring vat of boiling oil. On it goes from breakfast to lunch, when we get a breather. Then back we go until mid-afternoon Recreation, as things continue to heat up with the washing and ironing of a whole convent's-worth of laundry.

The basement of turbines and gears reminds me of those war movies depicting duty on a battle ship. Steel levers and cylinders and engines move machines to get the job done. When you start your Laundry stint, Sister Regina spends a day-long training session introducing the different machines, what they're for, and how to use them. Washers and dryers circle the sleeves and socks and aprons and what-all into view, and then away, in the glass doorways. Her machines gleam almost to blindness what with Sister Regina directing us to polish everything within an inch of its life every Friday.

Some of the equipment stands out. Take the press, for example. Standing waist-high, it's about four, maybe even five feet across. A giant, steaming iron. Its hot metal lid drops from above and clamps onto its padded tabletop when you press the activator button. Lay out some nun's gingham work apron on the pad; press the big round button. G-R-R-R—Down comes the hot jumbo iron in its steel arms, lands on the apron underneath, clamps down hard to press it flat-flat-flat. P-SH-OOOO—Steam sizzles all the way around from under the clenched lid. Then, press the button again before anything burns. KA-BAAAAM—The huge press flies like a bat off someone's work habit as its arms lift back up overhead. There's your habit, steaming and flat as a board.

Needless to say, it's challenging to stay on track with the litanies when you work the press. There, Sister Regina almost never gives you reminder pokes, because it's too easy to get distracted and burnt. What's fun is when you get your pressing going in a rhythm. Habit after habit after habit, the P-SH-OOOO-ing and KA-BAAAAM-ing sound off, regular as target-shooting. In no time, your flattened stuff stacks up like pancakes on the table to the side.

Rhythm is definitely key to mangling as well. But again, you want to be careful. The big and little mangles stand against one wall of the laundry—the big one wide enough to take an entire bedsheet through its steaming rollers. You need two people—say Sister Bernie and me—to get a rumpled sheet from the washer, pull it all the way out flat, and feed it through the rollers, keeping it tight and even between you until it comes out at the bottom of the hot-roller system, dry and smooth as paper.

Mangling sheets requires a coordinated warrior dance of bold movements. First, the two manglers pick up the damp sheet, then back away from each other in one move to spread it tight. In perfect timing, you feed the two sides into the rolling lips at the top of the big mangle. As the sheet journeys its way through the rollers, you each guide your side to keep the sheet angled and smooth until the lead-edge finishes its trip through the machine and starts getting spit out by the rollers at the bottom of the mangle. Maneuvering with precision, your feet dance as your fingers grip the corners of each about-to-be-mangled bed sheet while you move carefully to keep your long sleeves from getting fed along with it into the hot rolling spools.

Then when the mangled sheet makes it through, your synchronized mangling really picks up for the best part: pull tight, then crease the hot, smooth sheet between you, each with your arms spread wide holding the corners. Then scissor them together in a quick series of folds and refolds. Smooth as a circus act, every Wednesday Bernie and I work Mount Alverno's clean sheets through the big mangle. We stretch, feed, guide, pull, fold, and stack sheets and sheets and more sheets—a pair of mangling athletes. Meanwhile Sister Regina pokes smaller pillowcases and dishtowels through the little mangle and takes us through her litanies as we keep the beat: "Pray for us!" "Have mercy on us!" "Deliver us, O Lord!" "O God, Make haste to help us!"

Most of the ironing gets done machine-wise with the press and the mangles. Friday, being polishing-the-machines as well as underwear-day, requires almost no ironing at all. With one exception. The first time Sister Regina directs me to bring the ironing board down from the corner wall and then heat up the regular electric steam iron, I set it all up by the sunlit doorway. With the different saints flying around us in the litany, Sister Regina places a damp net bag of lingerie on the ironing board and nods toward the iron. "Gracious Holy Mother St. Claire," she hollers over the tumbling dryers. "Foundress of Convents of Holy Nuns for Our Blessed Father St. Francis."

"Pray for us!" I intone, as I turn the bag over and deposit its contents onto the board. Out fall some half-dozen pink, yellow, and lavender silk under-garments. I look back and forth between the lacey, frilly pile and the iron, now steaming and ready to go.

Pausing in mid-litany, Sister Regina hurries over to whisper: "Mother Priscilla's special bloomers. Press ve-e-ry, ve-e-ry carefully." With surprised resignation, I iron away as we ask the aid of any number of Franciscan saints devoted to poverty and asceticism, pressing the *be-jeebers* out of the fancy silk underwear of our Provincial Superior. Some things you discover in the laundry, you'd just as soon not know.

Out of the Furnace
and Up with the Frying Pans

MY CANONICAL YEAR CONTINUES intensely on the work front. When the stint with Bernie in the laundry is up, Sister Agatha posts new assignments for the next stretch. There I am, along with Sister Margie, in Sister Wilma's kitchen. A few months ago, Sister Wilma took over from Sister Marietta—whose jolly invitations to cigarette-smoking and *schnapps* on the rooftop under the stars I do miss.

Our work in the kitchen takes up almost the entire day, with three major productions plus snacks for afternoon Recreation to boot. Almost no time off until it's Compline. But, for all its long hours and hard work, Kitchen turns out to be more fun than Laundry. For one thing, even with giant ovens and burners and the hot electric vats for scrambling dozens and dozens of eggs all at once, the big workspace stays cooler. There in the middle of the whole sprawling set-up of convent buildings, its high, domed ceiling has skylight windows that you tilt open with a long stick, and a great, winged ceiling fan whirls peacefully to make the most of any breeze that slides through the windows.

Down beneath, Sister Wilma runs the kitchen, as quiet and even-tempered as the fan. She works out smooth plans for feeding every single nun at every meal in two dining rooms, one for the professed sisters and one for the novices. She loves getting the three of us—her and Margie and me—to dream up culinary surprises: orange and yellow nasturtiums sprinkled across vats of tossed salad; California grapefruit sections and avocadoes together in bowls smothered at the last moment with sparkling ginger ale; giant green peppers at the end of summer, baked chock-full of bacon and rice and green olives.

According to Sister Wilma, cooking is an adventure.

"Let's make every day a party. After all," she chuckles, "we've got a hundred and twenty people gathering together at our tables!"

It's also a challenge. We have to learn how to start up, then scramble and bake and fry with, and then shut down all the gigantic mixers, ovens, and stove tops that you need to make burgers or whatever it is for such a large, hungry crowd. But you get used to all the mechanical cooking devices. Bustling around with potholder gauntlets to turn the various wheels and shutters and cranks of machines that get a whole dinner ready can seem as exciting as landing a rocket ship. We three coordinate the food and the timing and the moves, poised to pull it all out of the oven in one grand flourish of carrying and scraping and spooning.

Just on the other side of the swinging doors at either end of our kitchen, Mother Priscilla and the professed sisters in the south refectory, and Sister Agatha and the novices and postulants in the north, sit with their eyes closed, listening contemplatively to the spiritual reading that precedes every meal. It's fun to live out the contrast on our side of the doors as we race around, filling up and positioning all our platters and pitchers and bowls in front of the shutters of the two serving windows, which will fling open after Mother Priscilla and Sister Agatha ring their little table bells to end the readings and bring on the food.

When we hear the bells, Margie and I each step into one of the two refectories to arrange what we've prepared in the proper order on the serving tables. Everything in its place, we each face the refectory's superior, give our solemn nod, and the little bells ring again to launch the meal. With the tinkling bells, boisterous talking fills each dining hall, as two attendant nuns fill plates at the serving tables and deliver them to the superiors. Then, in an orderly file, the cafeteria-style line-up begins as the rest go to serve their plates.

But from the kitchen Margie and I still have to bring out the *special* meals for various of the old, professed sisters: Sister Epiphania's chicken gruels and mushes because her false teeth aren't much for chewing; Sister Martina's separate bowls of meat, vegetables, and salad because of her blindness; Sister Regina's scrambled eggs and tortillas because, no matter what meal the rest of us are having, she will get sick if she tries to eat anything else.

Once we've carried out all the special trays to our special eaters, we only have to line up the desserts so they're poised for delivery at the next lifting of the kitchen's serving windows. When that's done, and the whole menu has gone out without a hitch, we three—me, Margie, and Sister Wilma—look at each other, smile with relief, hang our gingham aprons on the hooks inside the pantry, and head to our separate refectories to enjoy our day's cooking. It's usually pretty good. Sometimes even dashing—say with nasturtiums.

Another perk of the job: when your post is Kitchen, you *never* have to wash the dishes.

Stir Up Thy Might

Big dough… sweet dough… heaps of dough
    in Sister Wilma's kitchen.
It's quite something to stir
the mighty, metal, levered, hot or cold pot big as a barrel
that we use for everything—scrambling eggs, boiling pasta,
or just mixing stuff together
with its top-down, attachable electric mixer blade or,

                               without it,
with a wooden spoon as long as your arm.

> *Stir up thy might, O God, and save us.*
> *Give ear, O thou that rulest Israel.*
>
> (PSALM 79:2-3)

I'm at it now,
    beneath my shoveling
        a dozen eggs or so

a melted cornerstone of butter
pounds of flour
quarts of milk
brown sugar by the pitcher-loads
a pint of vanilla
cups of baking powder
a wee mound of salt.

Dig 'em and flip 'em
Roil 'em and tip 'em....

A giant mount of cookies-on-their-way
to feed the (might-as-well-be 5,000) hungry nuns.

Stir up thy might, O God...

But Sister Wilma's kitchen is fun.

For lo, she comes from the walk-in pantry
past the stand-up-inside-them coolers
and the expanse of griddles and ovens,
all five feet and seventy-something years of her
in her coverall gingham apron,

marching toward me and my giant steel pot,
making her face to shine,
each outstretched hand
waving a five-pound bag of chocolate chips
as she chants the morning's psalm:

Stir up thy might, O God,
Give chips, O thou that rulest Israel!

Island Retreat

IN LATE SUMMER WE novices have driven up to join some Dominican nuns for a week of silent retreat at their order's college in the hills above Santa Rosa—Dominican novices in white on one side of the chapel, Franciscans in brown on the other.

It's hot today. I've sat through one meditation, sermon, and prayer session too many and am making my way up the dirt road at the back of the chapel, before the next talk by Retreat Master Father Alfonso begins. Many retreatants take naps during afternoon sessions, so nobody will think twice if there's an empty spot in a Franciscan pew. I've wondered where this road leads ever since we arrived in our station wagons yesterday morning.

My white veil keeps the sun off my neck pretty well as I head up through the dry rocks and scrub that rise on either side as the little road winds into the hills. As soon as I get out of sight of the buildings, I set a steady pace for an afternoon's hike and roll up the sleeves of my habit above my elbows. Ah…cooler. My scapular flips and flops from side to side as I stride up the dusty road. Small brown birds jump in the sticks and grasses going up the canyon. A startled snake slithers across the dust in front of me and into a pile of rocks to the right.

For more than a year now I've been up at Mount Alverno and not gone anywhere by myself ever. A few times, when I was lonesome for the prairie, I snuck out on a full-moon night after Compline, careful that Sister Agatha not catch me. Climbing the back fence to the top part of the golf course on the other side, I'd scramble up and sit a while on the low branches of big trees to watch the moonlight gleam down the fairway. Ah-h-h-h! But not like heading out for a whole afternoon the way I did ever since being seven or eight, up north on our prairie where you could bicycle to the waterfalls below Gertrude's farm along the river, or gallop the horses across Henriots' fields and into the woods for a picnic lunch under the mossy oak trees by the pond.

I've never been near Santa Rosa before, and the college is way up in the hills above any houses or cities or golf courses. It's out in the country. A hot wind picks up as I march to the top of a rise and start down the other side. Everything widens out. Off in the distance, tree-covered hills stand against the sky as tawny hills between here and there roll out on all sides, divided by clusters of oak trees in ravines. Everything feels and smells and looks so *California*: it's exciting, like TV shows we watched at home in the rainy winters.

Walking in the hot sun, my feet crunch on the dirt road. Drops of sweat slide onto my forehead. Coming from up north, I don't like the heat much. The veil is going to have to go for now. Taking it off as I walk along, I carefully roll it over its little frame, then tuck it under the rope belt of my habit. My scapular continues to fly around with each step. My damp cropped hair jumps for joy in the wind. Hills covered with tall, yellow grasses shimmer around me.

The dirt road curves me up one hill and down the next. A whitish hawk circles overhead. I make it to the top of another rise in time to watch the bird float off over a grassy valley sprinkled with cattle. Way down below, a good-sized lake sparkles green and blue, with a wooded little island right in the middle. What a find on this hot day in this high-in-the-hills-place.

My pace picks up as I pass some gnarly oaks, then a stand of spicy-smelling eucalyptus trees, their cardboardy leaves rattling in the breeze. A path heads to the right, straight to the crusty dirt and swaying rushes that rim the lake.

The sun beats down. *Hot.* The little island sits quietly at the center of the sparkly water, just hopping with little brown birds in the blooms and grasses. Not a human sight or sound. I look out over the hills with their clusters of cows. H-m-m-m. Does anybody come around to see to these cows? Is there some kind of barn hidden up here somewhere? Some kind of ranch house? Some pickup truck driving around full of cowpunchers? Nothing but birds and cows to be seen anywhere.

At my back, the empty road winds down into the valley. I picture Sister Agatha, Father Alfonso and the whole herd of Franciscans and Dominicans stuck in their pews and dorm rooms way off behind me. I feel lucky. Has any other nun come out for a stroll and headed for the hills like me? The wind rustles over the lake, laps little waves onto the muddy shore. The sun's high overhead. Bugs buzz, land near the water, paddle around.

What are the chances of getting caught? My top teeth bite at my lower lip. Sweat tickles my cheek. The ferociously disapproving face of Sister Agatha floats into memory, until another hawk sails into view. Oh, hell. It's now or never.

My brown habit lands on a log at the shore—each item set down in a hasty order: shoes and knee-length stockings, brown habit, undershirt, underpants, scapular, coiled rope belt, and white veil at the top of the tidy pile. Quick as I can, I scamper into the lake, the slick mud squishing between my toes before I dive flat as soon as possible and slip naked into the cool water. Coming up for air, I turn to float on my back. Look in every direction. Then gaze up at the cloudless sky, the delicious water lapping about me.

I swim quietly through the rippling water toward the little island. Reaching its shore, I dart to a sheltered perch in some reeds to look around. Bees and bugs hum. Birds swoop, chatter and cheep. Now and then a cow hollers from one of the hillsides. My ears jump at the growl of an engine, fearing a pickup truck. Then I smile to recognize that it's skyward—a plane. Nobody's here but me. Another hawk floats overhead. I can just make out my rolled-up white veil on the log at the shore. How is this being a nun going to turn out?

Shadows from the island start to reach out onto the lake as the afternoon passes along. It must be time to swim back and habit up, then amble down the dirt road. Making my naked way from the water to my fully habited self takes a bit of a struggle as I wriggle clothes onto my wet body, worrying about possible passing cow-tenders. But it's only me and bugs and birds by the little lake.

As the sun lowers, I return quietly down the spindly road to slip back into the silence of white- and brown-clad nuns.

I make it in time for Vespers in the Dominicans' modern chapel followed by the silent dinner in the refectory. When night falls and it's Compline, a big orange moon rises over the round hills behind us. At the lake, crickets must be *chirring* as moonbeams jump across the water along with the stars.

The Voice of My Beloved Knocking

I sleep but my heart watcheth; the voice of my beloved knocking:
open to me, my sister, my love, my treasure—for my head
is full of dew, and my locks of the drops of the night.
(CANTICLE OF CANTICLES 5:2)

It doesn't hurt that the Bible puts it so well.

Sister Mary Clare crinkles her face,
        jokes with other novices,
        laughs and looks my way.

Mild winter night after Compline,
we slip outside—
forbidden, with Grand Silence begun.

The glorying moon huge,
and eucalyptus leaves rattling like castanets,
we talk about e.e. cummings, side-by-side on the stone wall,
inch closer . . . impossible not to take hands.

> *Honey and milk are under thy tongue,*
> *and the smell of thy garments as the smell of frankincense.*
>   (CANTICLE OF CANTICLES 4:11)

Uphill, the novitiate door bangs open
        and Sister Agatha, like a Fury
        hurtles toward us, stomps down the path,
        and breaches her Grand Silence with a furious hiss:
                "Sisters! To your cells THIS INSTANT!"

And so,
Mary Clare, older, already a second-year novice,
castigated, surveillanced,
eyes averted, avoids me.

But that voice knocks.

Months later, summer visitors fill the house,
and over refectory dishes,
Sister Julia from L.A. pauses,
        locks eyes.

        Watches for me at the edge of the cliff.

        Leaves a note buried in lilies near the bell tower.

Meets me breathless behind the garden wall,
  and in basement corridors,
  and beside the storage shed,

and after Compline
  as I ready things for tomorrow's breakfast,
  there, at the kitchen door,
  she knocks and beckons,
  with dewy locks, I'm sure.

What can we do but hurry into summer's moonlight—
fervent as fire, encompassing as rain?

  Who is she that comes forth as the morning rising,
   Fair as the moon, bright as the sun,
    Terrible as an army set in array?

        (CANTICLE OF CANTICLES 6:9)

Joy Moves On

DEEP TIME HOLDS US here as we live old, old patterns. But calendar time passes. The chrysanthemums and gardenias grow unruly at the base of the bell tower as I weed and prune for another two-month stint. With another summer, the birds are drunk again. Their tipsy selves plunge in loopy, chattering cannonballs off the tiles atop the tower.

Last year the spindly newborn fawn followed me around in my garden work, tiptoed on her narrow hooves, and nuzzled into the pockets of my apron looking for lettuce and carrot bits. She stayed for some months in the enclosed patios, and since then has been kept at the outskirts of the convent where she spends most of her time in the wilder far-off reaches of the mountain. She'll come at a run when I whistle or call out, "Joy." Mainly I whistle, as much like a birdcall as possible, since most of the time silence must be observed. Plus, I'm not crazy about her name.

A yearling now, she still joins us for evening Recreation as part of the community, strolling along the roadway that circles the grounds and the Spanish-style convent buildings. She usually walks with me, toward the back of the ambling procession, as Sisters Michele Marie, Elena, Leticia and the rest of the novices and postulants chatter away in their groups, always pleased by the break for talk between the long silent stretches of prayer and work.

But now that she's not really a fawn anymore, almost deer-size, the logistics of her monastic vocation have gotten harder to negotiate. Most days and nights she's off on her own—who knows where? I miss her as I tend my chrysanthemum patch, though she's not at all the innocent of last year who hovered near me, white-spotted and tottering about on her long legs, reaching out her little fawn-tongue with hopes of milk. Now she's apt to eat every plant in sight—flowering shrubs in the parking lot, leaves and branches and bark on the trees at the chapel entrance, even the weeds as I'm pulling and piling them in whatever part of the garden she finds me.

If she followed directions, she might fit in better. But, no. She's such a dear wild deer—mysterious and unpredictable. One day she's right here with me, the next—not a sign of her. At times she seems to listen: "Come on, babe. Here you are. This way, this way. Right here. That's it! You've got it, girl!" She stays next to me with what looks like successful training, until she doesn't. Or, we're in the garden, as peaceful and easy as Eden. Then Sister Somebody-Or-Other approaches, monastically silent and calm. No matter. Ears flick, nose twitches, eyes widen—off goes the panicked little doe, leaping wildly over bushes, ledges, walls, even wheelbarrows, shovels, hoes, or whatever else is in her way. In a flash, she's over the mountain's edge and down into the tangle of eucalyptus, rocks, and brush that cover the steep slope from our mountaintop to the streets and houses below.

I've trained dogs and horses. No rewards, no scoldings, no behavior modification can train this doe—not to come to me, not to move away from a treasured sapling, not to calm down and stop racing around a gaggle of nuns, not to stop munching every leaf in sight.

She still finds and follows me when the chance arises. "Well, Sister, if it isn't your little Postulant-in-Training!" Sister Sylvia laughingly announced

during yesterday's Recreation stroll when the little doe bounded up onto
the roadway to join us.

"Has she learned her Office chants yet?" Sister Jennifer quipped. No
hint of a smile appeared on the face of Novice Mistress Sister Agatha.
She's uttered more than a few warnings in my hearing about the deer's
"unruliness." The former fawn's days as a Franciscan are numbered. In my
own way, I've kept myself on the equivalent of the eucalyptus-edged cliff
of Sister Agatha's purview to avoid any final reckoning.

I lean the hoe against my bag of weed clumps and set out around the
bell tower searching for my furry troublemaker. I'd better make sure she's
not munching any more of Sister Noella's prize-winning roses. She got
a few of the Satin Beauties when I had her with me in the back patio on
Tuesday. Word came down: nothing of that sort to happen again. Dire
consequences.

The handyman, Mr. Roscoe Williams, comes sauntering across the
front parking lot. That usual good-natured smile crosses his sun-tanned
face under the rumpled fedora that tips jauntily to the left. "Howdy there,
Sister," he says as he walks up. "Nice mornin' to be out in the gardens." I
nod and smile, startled since I'm more used to silence than talking at this
time of day—wonder what's up. "Where's the deer?"

"I'm not sure." My throat catches.

"Mother Monica's directed me to fetch 'er up for a relocation out to
that wild game preserve out on the Crystal Springs highway."

My heart sinks.

"Can you find 'er and bring 'er out back where I've got the blue van,
so we can load 'er up?"

"Yes, sir, Mr. Williams," I mumble. "Be back there in a minute."

The sun hangs above the bell tower now as I walk down along the
eucalyptus grove toward the mountain's steep edge. It's perfectly overgrown
for munching and napping. I give a whistle. Softly call "Joy," then "Hey,
babe," and whistle again.

In her favorite spot—a grassy dip below the rim of slender trees, just before the cliff drops down—up goes her head, ears perked and wide. "Hey, there," I whisper, as she saunters up and pushes her nose under my gingham apron. I give her the usual pat and scratch her shoulder. I pause, take a breath, look far out over the hazy salt flats at the dwindling end of San Francisco Bay. Then we clamber up the rise and onto the road, the long, curving way around to the garage and the sheds at the back of the convent.

I trudge with short, heavy steps to where the truck must be waiting. The frisky little doe struts and hops along, ambles ahead, then circles back to urge me on with her nose, her pointy hooves tip-toeing on the warm asphalt. We stop to nuzzle one last time above the warm and busy hum of the South Bay. She nips at my fingers—probably dreaming of roses (or long-ago milk). We wend around the curve to the blue van parked beside Sister Noella's prize-winners, now temporarily barricaded behind a labyrinthine lattice of plastic fencing. Everything hangs thick and dusty. The grim, hot zing of the idling auto's engine drifts through the air and grabs at my nose.

Mr. Williams opens the sliding door and motions for me to get our overly wild wildlife into the van that will carry her off to the preserve. A little pen of tacked-together boards has been rigged up in the back to keep her from falling against the sides of the truck. Her ears twitch-twitch-twitch. Her nose sniffs and wheezes.

"Kind of skittish, ain't she?" Mr. Williams notes.

"It's okay, girl," I whisper softly, gently passing my hand over her side, calling on St. Francis, Saint of the Animals, for calm. Today is one of the days that she quiets down, slows her breathing, puts her face under my apron. More than most of her kind, she's used to moving in and out of un-forested human spaces—closets, patios, a volleyball court, the storage corner of the auto garage where she found me working one day. I crawl ahead of her into the makeshift pen with some lettuce, hum quietly, coax-and-pat-and-coax-and-pat. Trusting me, in she comes, joins me, gobbles up the lettuce, doesn't really seem to mind when I start backing out.

Leaning over her, I take in the sweet, peppery, furry smell. Whisper "Goodbye, Little One." Climbing out, I move back to the curb as Williams slams the sliding side door of the van. It latches with a clank. The little hooves tip-tip, tap-tap inside. He gets into the driver's seat, closes the door, shifts into gear. My heavy arm waves. The corner of my eye fills, then I taste the saltiness as the van rumbles up the hill and out the gate.

My afternoon drags on with listless weeding and hoeing. I picture the little doe jumping out of the clumsy, smelly van into a new big meadow brimming with tiny daisies and fellow deer. Two of their emissaries come to greet her, welcome her into the neighborhood. I'd be glad to see other creatures just like me and relieved to have new friends with four legs who like to eat bushes and flowers and trees like I do. Will she regale them with funny stories about her stout, two-legged sisters back on the mountain? Will she miss us? Wonder about seeing us again?

Or tell them about her early life as a Franciscan—her vocational difficulties—that odd-smelling hand and kind, whistling voice that brought milk; delicious roses; afternoon parades; that confusing, bouncing ride that brought her to the meadow?

Continuing Education

EVERYBODY KNOWS THAT SAN FRANCISCO is the center of just about everything and that Haight Street is the center of San Francisco. I can hardly believe it when a group of us novices start taking classes up in the City. After two years on Mount Alverno of trying to decipher the dull philosophy classes of Sister Celeste or the wacky theology of wall-eyed Father Aegidius, my career in a real college begins. And—lo and behold—the University of San Francisco campus and its beautiful spires of St. Ignatius sit only a few blocks uphill from where Haight Street meets the Golden Gate Park. We've gone from the remotest hilltop in the South Bay Area right to the Center of Everything.

Before dawn, a station wagon-load of us head off to the City on the Skyline Highway that twists its way over the top of the hills. Six of us jam into the Chevy, all habited for the outside world with our softer Sunday robes (brown, of course) and black veils instead of the novitiate white ones. Each has a satchel of notebooks and pens as well as the Office book and a sack from Sister Wilma's kitchen: a biscuit and fruit for breakfast, and a sandwich and cookie for lunch. While it's still almost night, one of us—usually Sister Kathy—drives us north for our day off the mountain. Saying the rosary starts us out. By the last stretch on our beads, after we've prayed our "Hail Marys" almost to the end, there we are along Crystal Springs Reservoir with the pink sky rippling in the water as the sea gulls ricochet around.

We come into the City from 19th Avenue, through Golden Gate Park and up Stanyan Street, then across the light at Fulton to the university. We stop at the Carmelite Convent across the street from campus for Mass at 6:00, and then each of us embarks on her school day. Because we've set out so early, chanting the Office has to be left to the novices and postulants and professed sisters back at the Motherhouse. Gone all day, each of us travelers prays her Hours silently at some version of the proper times. It's fun to figure out how and where to fit it in. Interesting quiet places present themselves—on the lawn by the arching fountain, at the top of the library, under a red bottlebrush tree in Golden Gate Park, and of course in Saint Ignatius Church on campus. There's a lot to be said for a sky filled with guiding saints and angels wherever you go.

Scheduling my classes gives me some headaches. The whole first day I stand in line, according to my now almost-never-used surname, in a gymnasium full of thousands of other college students. I don't have any idea how it works. The other novices disappear from view, buried in their own lines. All of a sudden, I'm here on my own at the giant university, even though all you see are faces. Bit by bit, the students in line for classes shuffle toward the folding table with its papers, cards, staplers, pencils, and very-busy-seated-people-in-glasses signing you up.

Finally, a stern grey-haired lady in a grey tweed suit takes my driver's license from home, my papers from the convent, and the list of classes Sister Emmeline typed up for us to present to the officials. "Let's see. How about a philosophy class, Sister?" "Yes, that sounds fine." "And beginning psychology?" "Okay." "What about English?" "Oh, yes please. I'd like two of those." "Let's see, we have 'English Romanticism' open. So far that fills

Mondays, Wednesdays, and Fridays. H-m-m, a poetry class meets in the mornings on Tuesdays and Thursdays. Do you want classes every day of the week, Sister?"

"Well, sure, I guess so." What has taken place exactly? I sigh with relief as I leave the folding table with my officially stamped list of classes. It takes pretty much all of registration day to (1) get lost a few times; (2) each time, find a signboard campus map for sorting that out; (3) locate the building where I stand in line to hand in the financial papers from Sister Emmeline; (4) locate another building to stand in a longer line for my library card; (5) locate the bookstore where I find my class books and stand in a long line to pay for them; and (6) finally remember to eat my lunch in a pew in the back of elegant Saint Ignatius before it's time to find the station wagon to drive back to Mount Alverno. Will I have any classes with my fellow Franciscans, Margie or Susan or Bridget or Yvonne? It turns out not, since I didn't know how to arrange it, with the alphabetized thousands of students lined up to enroll in the hundreds of classes a person might take. It's a long way from our prairie school, where eight of us graduated at the end of eighth-grade year.

So, it starts off with "Poetry." I locate the rundown second-floor classroom in an old brick building as it's filling up with girls and boys pretty much my age. Dressed in their V-necked sweaters, sneakers and blue-jeans, they file down the aisles of desks, carrying their red- and black- and green-strapped bookbags. I take a seat near the front. A fellow with short dark hair in the desk ahead turns around, looks at me, rolls his eyes, and motions to two shaggy-headed friends sitting nearby. "Time to relocate," he says, scrunching up his face. They all move across the room. Eventually a slight Asian girl in big glasses sits in front of me. The other desks nearby remain empty. Nobody seems to want to sit near "THE NUN." As the bell in the building clangs, hunched-over Father Athanasius totters into the stuffy room, sits down behind the big wooden desk at the front, and starts class.

It takes only a couple of class meetings to confirm a few things: (1) poetry itself is really fun, filling your head with sounds and pictures and ideas that go off in your mind like bursts of salty popcorn—this is not new information, since I grew up with my dad reading "Casey at the Bat" every summer and was writing my own poems by third grade; (2) Father Athanasius means well but hardly tells us anything I don't already know, and his way of saying it goes beyond tedious; and (3) the other students in class really don't like me. I sit down; the people nearby always get up and move. Overheard mumblings complain of "Sister Mary Smarty-Pants" and classes with "too many nunnies." One day, a freckle-faced guy with a crew-cut glares at me, then turns to say to a girl with a ponytail—obviously for me to hear—"Don't you hate when nuns horn in on *our* classes? All they do is raise the curve." Whatever that means…?

I blink. Where I come from, the nuns are some of the most respected people on the prairie. They teach schools and run hospitals. It never occurred to me that nuns would be treated rudely at college, of all places. In Psychology, Philosophy, and Romanticism—my big Monday-Wednesday-and-Friday auditorium classes, with professors at microphones—students sit next to me, but nobody talks to anybody. I'll never hear whether these hundreds of students like me or not. But on Tuesdays and Thursdays, the Chevy hauls me all the way to the City just so I can be bored to death by Father Athanasius, S.J., and harassed by a room of scornful students. Meanwhile, I can read Shakespeare's sonnets perfectly fine all by myself. By the second week I decide to adjust my Tuesday-Thursday schedule.

First thing after Thursday Mass at the Carmelites, I breakfast with my sack-lunch in St. Ignatius church, listening to the pipe organ. Then I race to arrive at "Poetry" early to get the seat by the door. The first few minutes give me the droning gist of Father A's lecture: what the poems are, what he thinks of them, what he wants us to do about it. Quick as a wink, I slip out the door. Down the creaky stairs. Out onto Fulton Street. Cross with the light at Stanyan. As the September sun climbs the morning sky, I stroll downhill to explore the famous Haight Street.

A cluster of long-haired people sit at the Stanyan Street entrance to Golden Gate Park. Three of them play guitars. A girl in a red bandana feeds the pigeons. On this side, a shirtless fellow in cut-offs and flip-flops stands in a doorway juggling three rolled-up boot-socks. Sunrays dapple the buildings as I amble along the sidewalk, my veil and scapular lifting in the breeze. For a second, I picture Father Athanasius and his uptight poetry students up the hill in that smelly old room, and smile.

At the corner of Haight Street, a bearded flute-player in a turban tootles away near a crimson door while the dog at his feet gnaws its paw. Overhead, sparrows *chirp* along on a wire like the chorus. Smells of spicy bread with cinnamon and cloves circle in another doorway, where a roly-poly woman with giant gold earrings grins and brings a tray of puffy buns to the counter as customers line up and look on. A bearded man in lime green with a crown of flowers smiles and waves: "Howdy-doody, Sister." Two women with long grey hair and elaborate jewelry even on their ankles and toes jaywalk across the street toward me, then enter the bakery. Exotic swirls of incense join the spices that follow me down the sidewalk. Everything sparkles with mirrors—sides of buildings, displays in shop windows, even people's clothes. Big and little wind chimes tinkle from windows.

More people than not wear robes and beads and veils. Nobody gives an ambling nun a second glance. No 'raising the curve' here. I stop and enter the Flying Fox Bookstore and Teashop.

"Well, well, well." A grey ponytail turns around, and a wrinkled face breaks into a grin. "What have we here? They call me Orion. Sagittarius with moon rising. And who might you be?" I look around. The small shop has no other visitors. Several shelves hold books. Two small tables stand near the window, their folding chairs waiting for tea drinkers. Next to me burns a gigantic candle, waist-high, some three feet across. Its wick of twisted rope lifts up into a long, dancing flame that licks toward the waxy inner walls, flickering variegations of red and peach and orange-gold along the sides.

"Pretty amazing candle," I sputter. Then, "I'm a Franciscan from Mount Alverno."

"Pleased to make your acquaintance." Mr. Orion bows. "Care for a cup of jasmine tea and some poems, Sister?"

I sit at the window table and watch the people strolling up and down the famous Haight Street. The jasmine tea swallows down just right, tasting like flowers in an old-fashioned cup-and-saucer that Mr. Orion fills from a flowery teapot. He brings over a slender book: *Otter Fancies* by someone named Starshine; publisher, Flying Fox Press, San Francisco. "A friend of mine, Starshine," he says as he sits in the folding chair opposite mine and puts on a pair of wire-rim glasses—nun-like, really. For the next patch of the afternoon Mr. Orion and I take turns reading funny little poems: "When You're Not a Rabbit"; "Spells of Purple Candle Mist"; "My Sister Moonshine, My Brother Sun"... almost Franciscan.

We reach the last page. I spy a clock on the wall—nearly 3:30.

"Gee. I'd best be going... got to get my ride."

"In the water, Sister Otter spins off and away; she'll swim down in her robes of brown on another day," he rhymes with a smile. "Here, you keep the poems." He puts the little volume into my hand.

"Th-thank you, Mr. Orion. Um-m-m...thank you very much," I stammer politely and stand to leave.

"Just call me Orion," he chuckles. "And Sister, you come back again, you hear?"

Out the door, I head west as the sun slips behind the park's towering evergreens. I scurry down Haight as other robed, veiled, and beaded passersby smile and step aside. "What a great poetry day," I think as I hurry up Stanyan to where the Chevy wagon waits at the Carmelite Convent. Tuesdays and Thursdays are all set.

College education takes off. Sister Kathy, older than the rest of us and already a nurse, knows a lot about the City because she used to live here. When the Big Earthquake struck in 1906, she says, the Sisters of Mercy from their hospital near 19th Avenue tended the devastated city so generously that the mayor and all the city officials passed a law: any nun can ride on city buses and trams and trains for free, in thanksgiving for the kindness of the Sisters of Mercy. Right away, I check to find out if that law still holds.

Next day, after keeping tabs on Father Athanasius, my first journey: down Geary to the old arcade called Playland at the Beach. I wait at the bus stop, trying to look as obviously like a nun as I can—kind of wise and well-mannered. A nearly empty bus heading west from campus stops for me. "Step up. Step up," the driver commands. "Good morning, Sister. Have a seat," he nods. Yup—it still works.

With metropolitan purpose, the rattling bus sways down the wide street to the Pacific Ocean. Sister Kathy highly recommends Playland, even though she says it's really dilapidated. Besides an ornate old merry-go-round, she described the world's best ice cream sandwich made *only* at two competing shops right at the ocean's edge. "Go to The Pie Shop or else The House of IT," she instructed. "Order an IT-Bar."

At the end of Geary, off I step into the windy sea mist, my scapular and veil swooshing about. The buildings and rides look rundown, the faded paint peeling down in stringy tatters. Ticket counters for some rides are open; not all of them. Boards cover the windows of closed-up shops. Only a couple of other visitors to Playland today. South, down the creaky boardwalk at the edge of the amusement park, side by side stand the rival shops. Here goes. I walk to the closed sliding window of the House of It and rap on a tattered sign: "ORDER HERE." A burly tattooed arm appears and opens the window.

"I wish to buy an IT-Bar, please."

A mustachioed man answers curtly, "Costs seventy-five cents." I place the coffee money I've been saving on the scruffy counter. Next thing I know, I'm eating my first IT-Bar: a fat center of vanilla ice cream sandwiched by two nubbly oatmeal cookies, the whole shebang encased in solid chocolate. Sister Kathy didn't steer me wrong.

I wander over to the deserted old carousel and study the prancing horses, my IT-Bar already in its last phase. "Care to ride, Sister?" another bulky tattooed fellow offers. "Off-season desperation prices: Nuns Go Free." The old guy chuckles and motions me on for a ride far longer than the merry-go-round at the Lewis County Fair ever gave me, even on my birthday.

Being a nun has real advantages in San Francisco, no matter how "Poetry" students behave. I smile as I bus my way back to the parked Chevy at the Carmelite Convent.

My education continues through the term. Even in the rain, whole days carry me by bus or tram from one end of the City to the other: bustling Market Street; down by Mission Dolores where I look up at the palm trees and stop in at the church to pray my morning Hours; past bank after bank on Montgomery; on to North Beach with the topless bars and Italian groceries but no beatniks that I can see; Chinatown, its market doorways hanging with plucked chickens and ducks and jingling chimes; Fisherman's Wharf and its bread smells and crab shops; out to the Sunset District with its rows of houses, ballfields, and churches; Golden Gate Park with its gardens, pavilions, and lakes; all the way along the ocean as far as the Zoo. San Francisco is a long way from Cowlitz Prairie, Washington.

Every now and then, I return to The Flying Fox to drink tea and read poetry with Orion. For the sake of Shakespeare and Emily Dickinson, I keep my hand in with Father Athanasius and put up with the snarly-minded students.

To this day, when I have a hard time over anything, I can close my eyes and picture standing on the outside ledge of the Powell Street Cable Car.

It lifts and creaks itself up out of Chinatown. Thrillingly, it drops from the rim of the hill and tumbles straight down for blocks and blocks to Fisherman's Wharf. Like a turning kaleidoscope, the City's bright roofs and towers and the whole wide and shining San Francisco Bay sparkle below. Me? I tightly grip the worn metal of the car's standing post with one hand. Cable- and brake-smells zip through the air. My other hand holds onto my black veil, which is whipping every which way it can around my head.

Bend the Stubborn

People of rank, how long will your hearts be dull?
Why do you love what is vain, and seek after falsehood?

I've about had it with things around here,
    What with the shiny fleet of V-8 Chevys and Buicks,
    the luxury-latter reserved for the bigwigs
                    (or rather BigWimples).

    Meanwhile,
    the postulants hazard their lives
    to ferry our librarian Miss Pitcairn back and forth
    from her little apartment in Woodside
        in a tiny, rattling Fiat
            whose transmission barely makes it to fourth gear.

So, where's the Franciscan in that?

And Saint Francis loved the animals,
      yet the whole Motherhouse office prickled with rancor
          because a motherless fawn
          ate a few roses.

And need mention be made
of Mother Priscilla's silk bloomers
      and their need to be ironed
      (as opposed to the ragged cotton undies of everyone else)?

People of rank!

Would Saint Francis not be shaking a finger
                    or maybe a fist?

        Bend the stubborn heart and will,
        Melt the frozen, warm the chill.
            (SEQUENCE FOR PENTECOST: 22-23)

My ceremony of vows happens next summer—
poverty, chastity, obedience.

Forever.

Can I really sign on for this thing?

Striding On

THE BLACK GRANNY SHOES of my Franciscan habit feel so sturdy and akin to my cowboy boots back in the old days on the prairie. The laces tie up snugly all the way above my ankles, and they've got wide heels with even a bit more of a lift than my boots. Even if they are old-fashioned, they carry me in a stride—that's what it is. It's important to stride because it gives you confidence and, of course, good speed as you make your way from one place to the next.

Right now, I'm by myself, striding around the big hilltop drive that circles the Motherhouse. It's mid-December. Classes in San Francisco are done, and I've almost finished writing my exams and papers. The sun has shone bright and crisp all day. As Sister Delphine's crew of one, I finished early with the floor-polisher that brought the corridors in the professed sisters' wing to an eye-cracking gleam. After covering the halls with wax, I whisked the three-speed machine over those floors, brushing the linoleum to blazing in record time. Changed into my soft dress-up habit now from my rough denim and gingham apron, I still have time for a pre-lunch stroll.

The December wind whips my white novice-veil about as I reach the cliff-edge and look far down to the south end of the bay and the brown peaks beyond. I start wondering what courses I might take at the University of San Francisco next term. Philosophy? Literature? Maybe music? The breeze lifts the outer brown scapular of my habit like a crazy sail luffing in front and behind. It feels great to have the wind fill your habit fore and aft—real energy speeds you along, like wearing red-tail hawk feathers. Anything's possible!

Coming to the end of my stroll near the chapel, I go in a side door, thinking about lunch. Now the scapular barely rustles with my calm stride down the corridor. I pass the office of Sister Dorothy, our new Novice Mistress.

"Sister," her voice calls from within the little office.

I stop. My granny shoes back me in reverse to her open door. The recent change from Sister Agatha to Sister Dorothy as our in-charge suits me fine. From the time I arrived, I had been holding my breath and tip-toeing to avoid the frowns and grumpy castigations of Sister Agatha. Sister Dorothy, however, laughs easily about things and looks for what you've done well.

"Yes, Sister Dorothy." I peer into the doorway.

"Please come in and sit down, Sister." She beckons to the chair in front of her desk. "I want to talk with you about something."

Her pale-blue eyes widen a little above her smile as I sit down. Outside the window, the winter-pruned stalks of Sister Noella's bushes line the beds of the interior patio, waiting to sprout their prize-winning buds when Easter comes. These days no little fawn lunches about on Mount Alverno, threatening our blue-ribbon roses.

"As you prepare to take vows in August," she begins, "we want you to experience convent life in a setting apart from the monasticism here at the Motherhouse. How would you like to move to one of our convents and work in community there—say, teach or do social work for a parish?"

I inhale, blink, take a long, slow breath. Yes, the vows coming up. In a flash a post-vows future jumps up, affixes me permanently as a Franciscan in this province. Since I'm not interested in nursing, I'll be teaching in the various schools sprinkled from Seattle south to Los Angeles. I focus on what Sister Dorothy's just said.

"M-m-m. Well, sure." I nod, folding my scapular on my lap and wondering what exactly I'm sort of agreeing to. (One thing I know after three years of being a nun—when you're told you're going somewhere, you'll be going there.) Stunned, my mind doesn't come up with anything more to say.

"Good," she replies quickly. "I'll put you on the list, and we'll talk soon. How's that?"

"Fine. Okay," I mumble. "Thank you, Sister Dorothy. Good afternoon, Sister. Good afternoon." My thoughts tangle and tumble as I head back outside. Where? Who else? Doing what? Suddenly I want to do more striding along the cliff before the bells toll for lunch.

Later that afternoon, after typing up the final versions of my term papers, I'm outside again. Far below, the Stanford tower shimmers pink in the afternoon sun, and I take in the fact that I won't be going back to USF in the City. Where will I be? My heart jumps, until the bells in tower tell me to make my way up the hill to the chanting calm of Vespers.

The next day after breakfast, Sister Dorothy follows me out of the refectory and walks me to her office for the next part of our conversation—well, hers, anyway.

"Mother Priscilla, Sister Ursula, Sister Emmeline, and I have a plan," she smiles. "And it's all arranged."

"U-m-m, good," I gulp, as I drop to the office chair to hear the rest of my plan.

Right after Christmas, I'll be in the station wagon of the sisters from the Portland convent. After their holiday visit to Mount Alverno, I'll drive back north with them to begin the second half of the teaching year at the parish grammar school. My assignment: (1) become the music program for grades one through eight of Assumption school, where they haven't had a note of music since the lay teacher quit four years ago; and (2) take stock (to myself) about my vocation and the vows I'm scheduled to swear to at summer's end.

Okay, then. To myself, I admit that I have serious doubts about the durability of my convent vocation. However, I do need to check it out thoroughly. Also, I feel good about going to teach so I can contribute to the order, return to them some payment and thanks for the education I've been given these past few years—getting to know so much of the library from Miss Pitcairn, bottle-feeding little Joy until she was following me around everywhere, surviving Father Aegidius but learning how the liturgy works, taking care of all the cars, whipping the polishers around the corridors with Sister Delphine, cooking on a grand scale with Sister Wilma, and especially getting to study at the university in the City.

Two days after Christmas, the beige Chevy wagon speeds up the noisy Bayshore Highway to begin the journey from California to the northern edge of Oregon. My little suitcase lines up in the back with the others. It holds my other dress-up habit and an extra black veil like what I have on, not novice-white (part of trying out being a full-fledged professed sister). Also in there are my brown denim work habit, my black canvas tennis shoes, my sandals, two nightgowns, knee-socks, underwear, and handkerchiefs. Of course, my breviary nestles in, along with a slim book of e.e. cummings that Sister Julia gave me last summer, a small New Testament, a book of folk songs, and some Bach and Mozart. My guitar in its case rides on top of the suitcases. Mother Priscilla and the others decided that, since I play the organ in chapel for Mass and the piano for fun, strum the guitar and banjo every chance I get, and organize all the guitar Mass liturgies and song sheets for Mount Alverno, I should be able to set up a music program at Assumption School.

The first day's trip will be just a few hours after lunch to the convent in Sacramento, where we'll stay the night. Until now, I've never met the four professed nuns from Portland, members of my new community: Mother Isabel (the Superior), Sister Martin Marie, Sister Gemma, and Sister Rosalie. They teach different grade levels at Assumption. Sister Leticia, who teaches at the high school in Sacramento, is along for the ride that far. Three in front, three in back.

At first there's a bit of talk, especially in the front seat—about the holiday, the weather, the traffic, the route, people in the Portland parish I don't know; but with a hummingbird whirring where my heart should be, I hardly hear anything anyone's saying. My black cape wrapped around me, and my head leaning back on my guitar case, I complete the backseat trio, silently watching cars and buildings fly by outside the windows. By the time we're onto the Bay Bridge, Mother Isabel clicks the radio on to some loud easy-listening channel. At the oak-sprinkled hills beyond Vallejo, lavish strings violin their way through "Some Enchanted Evening." At least when university buildings in Berkeley went by a while ago, "The Blue Danube" played.

We reach Sacramento and arrive at St. Francis Convent in time for Vespers, then have dinner. I visit a little with Sisters Denise and Mary Francis, who graduated high school a few years before me on the prairie and now teach in the grade school here. Since they were several years older, I never knew them well and stab around at the conversation.

"Do you like teaching?"

"Very much," they say. Third grade boys chase crickets, and fifth graders vie to be best at neatening the book cupboard.

"Does it get hot in the summer in Sacramento?"

"Oh, dreadfully," Sister Mary Francis declares. "But then, we spend most of the summer living at one of the convents in LA, to take college classes for our teaching degrees."

"Well, do you have any ideas for how to set up a music program for a grammar school?"

"Well, not really." They both laugh. "But what an adventure you'll have!"

Sister Denise adds, "Don't worry. It'll be just fine." I'm not so sure. But they come across happy enough. As everyone chatters during the Hour of Recreation, I can't wait for the Grand Silence that begins with the Compline bell for chanting, and then bed. At the moment, this adventure feels pretty uncomfortable.

Next morning, we start off right after Lauds and the silent Friday breakfast of cornflakes and coffee. The long drive into the mountains and north through the peaks and valleys of Oregon speeds by way too fast— even stashed in the middle of three across-the-backseat nuns.

Several packed sandwiches with potato chips later, by nightfall we've crossed the bridge into southeast Portland. Coming up a short street past the dark spire of a church, the Chevy enters a big asphalt parking lot that turns into a playground. Behind it, a rambling one-story brick grade school gleams an odd pea-green beneath high, glaring lights posted all across the lot. Slowly passing a forlorn, string-less basketball hoop, the Chevy noses its way to park beside the red-brick convent, a separate, boxy two-story building off to the back, also lit harshly pea-green. A dark, forested hill rises steep and stern at the back of it all.

"Well, here we are," announces Mother Isabel with a sigh. We clamber out and retrieve our luggage.

As I stand in the convent entry, guitar case in one hand, suitcase in the other, she comes up to me: "Sister Martin Marie will show you upstairs to your room, Sister. Just follow her."

We pass a small kitchen, a large dining-room table visible in the next room. The linoleum floor has seen better days, its white now eggshell, its faded tulips barely discernible in the fluorescent light. We ascend to the second floor where closed doors to bedrooms line the carpeted hallway. Three rooms down, we stop at an open door where light from the parking lot through the window casts the same pea-green onto the room's little desk, knotty-pine chest of drawers, and made-up bed. Martin Marie switches on the desk lamp, then closes the plaid curtains. "Well, here you are, Sister."

"Thank you." I take a deep breath and set my suitcase on the bed.

"We'll gather in ten minutes for night prayers," she tells me. "In the chapel down the stairs at the far end of the hall. Welcome to Assumption," she smiles, moving toward the door. "We'll be in Grand Silence for the night, but just knock at the next room if you have any questions, ok?... Oh," she turns and smiles as she leaves, "and call me Martie."

The door closes behind her.

Putting my guitar under the window, I quickly unpack: clothes in the closet, books on the desk, and suitcase under the bed. Taking my breviary for Compline, I stop by the tidy, shared bathroom on the way, then descend the far stairs to find the chapel.

As I step from the stairway, light brightens a doorway just ahead, and I enter the modest, pale pink room that serves as chapel. A good-sized crucifix hangs on the wall above and behind the small altar for Mass, its white cloths in place and two candles unlit for now. To the right, a red sanctuary lamp drops from the ceiling, the flame jumping in its glass. The pasty pink walls seem to mute everything in the not-very-chapel-like chapel. A painted statue of the Blessed Virgin, maybe two feet tall, stands off to the side on a little brown table, flames in three vigil lights bobbing at her feet. At the front of the altar are scattered a collection of small, single-kneeler prie-dieux of different designs, each with a chair and a single shelf holding a breviary and prayer books. Mother Isabel nods toward an empty one at the back where I take my place, kneel, and open my breviary to today's Compline, eager for the familiar chanting.

Looking around after some minutes, I realize that each nun at her kneeler is silently leafing through the Hour of Compline on her own. No chanting of the Hours at Assumption Convent? I dutifully thumb through night prayer along with my chant-less little new community, my heart heavy. It doesn't take long at all when you're reading through Compline by yourself.

Finishing my prayers, I slip out of the pink chapel. A by-now familiar pea-green shaft streams down at the far end of the hall. I tiptoe to a win-dowed doorway that looks out on a back porch and stand at the shadow side of the window. With barely a sound, I delicately unlock the door, turning the knob with my right hand under the bunched-up, muffling scapular in my left. I coax the door open, step onto the porch, and care-fully close it—unlocked. Alone on the little porch, I hear distant cars on night-time city streets, see a half-moon high among dim stars, and find the Big Dipper in the sky to the right. The mysterious dark forest rises steep along the backside of the convent, the school, the church and their grim parking lot.

Another deep breath. Evergreen branches rustle in a momentary drift of wind. From the dark forest: *Whoo-whoo—whooo.*

An owl! I haven't heard an owl hooting since I was on the prairie.

I stand in the moonlight listening as long as I can hold out in the cold. Then stealthily I slip back inside, locking the door without a sound. Leaning down, I untie and slip off my granny-shoes, take them in hand and tip-toe past the chapel and up the stairs to my room.

Help!

THURSDAY-BEFORE-LUNCH STARTS out as a good idea. There we are as usual: me rapping on the classroom door at 11:15, them finishing their grammar lesson. Sister Gemma opens the door and motions the class to rise. With a shuffling hub-bub, the ragged chorus stands by their desks to greet me: "Good mor—ning, Si—ster."

"Good morning, seventh graders," I reply, my guitar case knocking the folds of my habit against my knee as I step in. Gathering books and papers from her desk, Sister Gemma exits as I enter.

This seventh grade is my last class on Thursdays before the lunch bell. My guitar and I—the school's music program—go from room to room all week, to the two classrooms for each grade, one through eight. I work out songs and ditties to teach skills in voice and listening: harmony and counterpoint; singing antiphonally, with various parts of a room coming in at different times; rhythmic flourishes with clapping, sticks, and tambourines. We go from "Old McDonald" and my settings of Dr. Seuss rhymes for first and second graders, to harmonies and part-singing on Mozart canons and answer-back folk and rock songs for the big kids. I accompany with piano or guitar unless we're singing a capella. If a big feast is upcoming, we do church pieces and Mass parts, otherwise it's mainly "This Land Is Your Land," "Froggy Went A-Courting," "America the Beautiful," "Take Me Out to the Ball Game," and for the older kids, popular songs by the Beatles and Bob Dylan.

Seventh graders inevitably drag their feet. They're not far beyond the fifth and sixth graders in skill and experience, but their willingness could fit into a thimble—and most are convinced their next stop is Broadway or Fillmore West. Maybe it's hormones. Assumption Elementary is my first teaching, apart from showing younger siblings how to read or giving piano lessons to Howie McNelly's little sisters when I was in high school. A lot of the time here it's fun. But both seventh-grade classes take the cake for "uncooperative," and Sister Gemma's gets the bakery's top prize.

May sunbeams pour through the open windows. "How 'bout we have class outside on such a pretty day?" Of course, they're all for it. With a melee of scraping desks, bookbags, purses, and jackets, off we go. Down the dark hall, through the double-glass entrance doors, they traipse up the hill to the sunlit knoll at the back of the building.

"Okay. On the grass. Into a semi-circle, everyone."

This week's lesson: how to sing counter-melodies and harmony as they enter a song in overlapping places. Today, it's "Help!" by The Beatles. The early morning class learned it, and hearing themselves singing in parts impressed them, even the boys.

Seventh-grade skepticism circulates as usual. My typed-up and multi-copied word sheets flutter from student hand to student hand as I go over what will happen. Questions arise. When to come in? Who gets which parts? What if they'd rather sing another part? What if they might be getting laryngitis? My answers: I'll give the cues for entrances; boys sing lower parts, girls sing over them; everyone who wants a passing grade will sing; anyone sick should go to the infirmary. Despite their best efforts to stall, a plan for singing "Help!" in counterpoint slithers into place.

"Okay, girls, on this side." I motion right. Scuffling about, they rise and move as directed, after considerable brushing and checking of uniforms for clinging grass and twigs.

"Boys, on the left." I point toward the trunk of a nut tree nearby— maybe some kind of walnut. Pulling taffy comes to mind as I strive to maneuver their wiggling more or less into a semicircle near the tree. I slip the strap over my head, strum, and model the girls' opening lines: *"When I was younger, so much younger than today, / I never needed anybody's help in any way."* (They must be picturing themselves at four or five—just as I think back to myself at their age, twelve or thirteen, picking up and figuring out how to play guitar, riding around the prairie, or taking the horses down to the river). In no time, they learn their whole part for the song. "Great! Let's give it a go with the boys?" They nod, a few even looking eager.

"*Only you* can supply the grounding for the whole song," I assure the frowning boys. "Your lower, slower lines come in *after* and *below* the girls' part."

They look dubious.

"Okay, guys, listen to your part. Don't worry—it's fun. Especially when everyone comes in together and hollers *"Help!"*

The opening: *"Wh-e-e-e-n—I was young—ne-ver n-ee-ded."* It's not exactly what's on the recording, which I don't have, just kind of remember. But it captures the idea. I have them sing it several times. Reluctant and tunefully impressionistic, their gloomy growling will work fine once we patch in the parts. We make our way phrase-by-phrase through the various sung entrances for the boys. "Yeah, that'll do," I smile encouragingly. "Let's put it all together."

A bold opening guitar chord changes to another, pauses as a cue, and I bring them in, singing with them. *"Whe-e-e-n,"* the boys begin with gravelly voices. Immediately the girls follow, lilting in over them: *"When I was younger, so much younger than today."*

Sunlight dapples through the leaves and over the seventh graders sitting on the lawn. The boys come in with some fine low groaning on their next entrance: "*But now—I've changed*," as the girls pipe above them: "*But now I find, I've changed my mind.*" Cars down on 82nd Avenue and Stark stop and start, the alternating hum and splutter of their engines spaced by the changing traffic lights. Giddy sparrows and robins chatter about springtime above the motor din.

At the chorus, I stop to coach the girls. "*Help! I need somebody*," I sing, turning away from the ten or twelve boys sprawled in the shadows. Why does my stomach jump?

In the last row, Megan and Lisa look startled and back up gingerly against the brick wall behind them. The girls and I sing, striving to fit voices, words, and notes. More-than-the-usual rustlings accompany our high-pitched "*Help!*"

The entire back row of girls—Megan, Lisa, Jeannie, and more—crouches behind those in front, squealing to our tuneful "*Help!*"s.

Pelt... plop... pelt. Missiles drop from the spreading branches. Spindly corduroy pant legs ending in sneakers dangle ominously from the newly unfurled leaves.

With teacherly attention directed to the girls, the limited good conduct of well known troublemakers Jim and Joe O'Connell has elapsed. Always lurking at the back, the lanky twins have snuck into the tree to dispense what's left of last year's nuts onto the girls—who stoically strive to maintain decorum. Keeping eyes on me, the girls huddle, tug their sweaters close, and gamely continue their singing. The remaining boys on the grass squiggle into subgroups of greater or less collusion in the too-close-to-lunchtime, too-out-in-nature revolt.

The song devolves into halting and vestigial "*Help!*"s amid twigs, leaves, and crusty old nut-bits pelting the squirming and dodging gaggle of students. "*Help!*" You can say that again.

If my career in teaching continues—and it will—this is the last time a class of mine journeys into the hormonal outdoor mayhem of spring.

I strike a furious chord.

"James and Joseph O'Connell! Down from that tree this instant!" The scrumming in the grass halts. Nothing but the distant traffic.

From upper branches, a scattering of formerly-intended missiles dribbles down the trunk. Four sneakers followed by corduroy pant legs clumsily descend from branch to branch, then drop to the ground.

Mortified at my own desperate outburst, I breathe deep, stare them up and down, pull myself to full height, and demand an apology. Twinned blond heads bow in remorse. Almost in harmony, a mumbled "S-o-o-o-r-r-r-r-y." First to me. Then to the class.

The bell clangs a release.

"T-t-t-to l-l-l-lunch," I stammer fiercely, flinging my arm in the direction of the school. Seventh grade disperses in silence.

I wait in the shade of the nut tree. Long to climb it myself. Strum a few chords. Stop. Listen to the traffic. Pack my guitar in its case along with my satchel of song sheets. Arrive late at the convent dining room for tuna sandwiches and tomato soup.

My afternoon features the little kids and "The Old Lady Who Swallowed the Fly."

Out of the Mire

… God heard my prayers and brought me
out of the pit of misery and the mire of dregs,
and set my feet upon a rock and directed my steps
and put a new canticle into my mouth …

(PSALM 39:3-4)

What's next … how can you know?
But it gets easier to tell …
       Knowing myself here,
       knowing here, in each here,
          picturing not here.

Setting my feet on the rock
       I look and listen,
hearing sounds that call
       or maybe warn,

watching the wind blow,
catching what trees have to say,
     like the scent of eucalyptus
         floating down after a rain,
         or the incense whiff of cedars
            circling the limbs in damp forests
     and spicy kinnikinnik
         out along the ground.
I know now:
     you can follow where you're led,
     unless you try too hard to think about it.

Will you go, lassie?
Will you go?

On High

MICHAEL, YOUNGER BROTHER OF Novice Mistress Sister Dorothy, came by yesterday from California for a stopover on his way to visit friends in Seattle. As he was leaving after lunch, he motioned me to his red top-down convertible, opened the glove box, and from it took a packet of greetings from Mount Alverno. Then, a pack of Marlboros and a marijuana joint as thick as my finger. Handing them off with a wink, "Enjoy," he chuckled, then climbed in and drove off in a roar and a puff of smoke.

My surprising new stash, held tightly in one hand, goes first under the scapular of my habit that drapes to my knees, and then upstairs to my cell. Quickly shove the smokes under a camouflaging heap of paper and envelopes in the back of the desk's lower drawer, then read the several notes from friends.

The smokes stay on my mind during the afternoon's classes as I instruct squirming six-year-olds and resistant pre-teens to sing, then later as I read the psalms and Magnificat of the afternoon Vespers. The birds chatter and sing about sunset coming on. How about this golden evening for a smoke?

Upstairs after dinner to retrieve the little bag, I see Sister Martin Marie's door ajar and give a tap-tap. "Want to climb up Mount Tabor butte for the sunset?"

"Sure," she nods. Martie has been my best pal and confidante here at Assumption, always ready for adventure—really, the only one in the little community of nuns I've felt at home with. She teaches one of the two big sixth-grade classes, and we've been collaborating the whole time on guitar Masses, visiting food pantries, working with ragged and renegade teens at the Eastside Center, sympathizing with oppressed and troubled parish women. We put together an end-of-the-year music and dance program for the Assumption school and parish community, to the theme of Stravinsky's "Firebird Suite" that included kids from first grade on up. Even the know-it-all seventh- and eighth-grade boys got involved building props and making a lightshow backdrop, with slide projectors that beamed through glass baking-pans of food coloring bubbling in olive oil. "Far out" we all learned to say, as wild light-shapes swirled across the ceiling and walls of the cafeteria that was our performance hall—Assumption's own Fillmore West. Martie is up for anything.

By this Friday, just before the last week of school, the days have grown long, and not just for the students. But, shadows now cover the school building and the convent house, backed right underneath the steep evergreen forest of Mount Tabor Park to the west. And my decision's been made. In a few weeks, I'll say good-bye to this parish and school, catch a ride back to Mount Alverno Motherhouse to pack up my few things there, and close my life's Franciscan convent chapter.

With no idea what's next.

Martie and I walk out the convent's back gate to the park entrance just beyond. The low sun throws a halo around the Mount. A steep trail zig-zags up through the forest; nun shoes aren't bad for hiking. As we climb higher, shafts of warm twilight glint through the looming evergreens.

Oranges and pinks filter overhead until, huffing and puffing, we reach the top of the butte.

Park fields and gardens open out beneath us. Far below, a reservoir with its splashing fountain reflects the sunset. Walkways surround the rippling water and stretch across the grassy park. Up on this more visited, city side of the Mount, benches stand here and there.

Night begins turning on all the lights—shop signs and gas stations in reds and blues and greens, yellow windows one-by-one flickering in houses. Car lights start blinking back and forth along the streets—yellow coming toward us from the bridges that connect to downtown; red going away toward the river. High windows and neon signs sparkle many stories up.

"Well, Sister Martie," I clear my throat. "Any interest in a little smoke, in honor of the almost end of our school year?"

Turning, she lets out a squeal. "Shoot, Sister! You do come up with extracurricular activities, don't you?" Next, "Sure. What've you got?"

I pull the Marlboros from the pocket of my habit. Then, with dramatic flourish, the joint. "This will be a first." I grin, waving the aromatic marijuana around her nose, then returning it to my pocket as we continue walking.

"My Lord. Where'd those come from?"

Of course, in the normal course of things, strictly proper nuns don't smoke. But Martie knows about my rooftop cigarettes with Sister Marietta back at Mount Alverno. And every so often she and I would accept a light from the rambunctious teens playing pool with us at the Eastside Center. Tossing my scapular over my shoulder, I'd try to act cool, inhaling a puff or two before putting my cigarette in an ashtray and aiming my cue in hopes of sinking a shot.

Now, at the top of the butte, we amble along the edge of the forest on a path that loops around, then winds down toward the pool and the grassy park and city below.

I stop. "Let's stay up here and watch the lights and stars."

Assumption Parish School has had its good parts—creating music classes, singing with all the elementary-school kids; playing guitar Masses for the big parish; getting to know Martie; hanging out and trying to help the tough teens on the Eastside. But mainly I got to realize that I can't do this for my whole life.

We come to a bench, just before the path turns down. "Let's stay here."

A pale sliver of moon floats over the city. We sit side by side, and I talk as Martie listens, about leaving Portland and saying goodbye to convent life altogether. The dewy night air smells sweet—spring grass, rich dirt and new roses just below, recently rained-on pines and firs above. I squint, looking for stars in the darkening sky.

After a long silence—"You'll be so missed," Martie whispers, then puts her arm around my shoulder, kisses my cheek. My throat catches, and my eyes water at the corners.

"It's ... um-m-m ... been in the works for a while now. I mean ... uh-h-h ... I've known it has to happen ... even though—everything on ahead seems anything but certain." I hate trying to make sense of complicated things. Look up, blink, see more stars faintly showing themselves. Night's really coming on now. The moon slips behind the far hills. City lights twinkle everywhere. I give myself a shake... don't want to think beyond tonight. No one but us anywhere in this park.

"Ever smoke weed?" I reach into my pocket.

"Of course not."

"Me neither."

"Well, isn't it about time we join the modern age?" She giggles.

"H-m-m-m-m."

"So, how's it go?"

"Like any smoke, I s'pose... just wait longer to exhale, so whatever happens has plenty of time to happen."

"How hard can it be?" we say in tandem, and laugh.

I light up. With the whole city twinkling before us, our thick little joint passes back and forth on the bench at the top of the butte.

"I wonder what happens."

"Dunno. Feeling any different?"

"Not really. I do feel kind of hungry."

"Me too, now that you mention it. Guess we'll have to make do with Marlboros."

When the joint's smoked down, I light us a cigarette apiece.

The hum of the city seems to get louder and louder, almost musical. The smoke and spicy smell drape a comforting blanket over our solitary bench. Like fireworks, the lights below and across start hopping and jumping every which way. Venus gleams over the city as the sky bubbles overhead with stars. Streaming head- and taillights thread their way back and forth over the row of bridges. On the far hills beyond the downtown, each radio and television tower serially explodes its silent, crimson lights: bottom-blink—middle-blink—top-blink…. bottom-blink—middle-blink—top-blink … fuzzy-edged light-balloons leap-frogging over and over.

"Guess I must be a little stoned." The tangerine-colored ash tip of my cigarette slowly taps itself onto the gravel path. I take a deep breath as I watch it fall. Silently ask it where I'm headed next. Back down the other side of this butte, I guess. Even that seems like kind of a tall order. "S'pose we better start down."

"Sure. I really do wish we had something to eat."

"Yeah—didn't think of that. A GIANT strawberry milkshake!"

We both sigh and laugh.

Martie gives a little cough. Stamps out her cigarette.

Bedazzled, we rise from our bench, stagger slightly, and stumble to the top of the hill. With a look back at the psychedelically blossoming lights of the city, we turn and begin to pick our way down what eerily appears as an on-again, off-again path through the woods. My arm gets tangled up in my scapular, so I toss the front part over my shoulder and out of the way. As our feet feel their way along the gravel trail, shadows loom before us as if the firs magically acquire more branches even as we watch. To make matters worse, my eyes seem to get stuck on them one after the other. In seeming slow motion, we zig-zag our way down the east side of the butte along a path that meanders from ghost-tree to ghost-tree. We know where we're going, unless we try to think about it.

Was this a good idea?

Suddenly, the neighborhood emerges as a recognizable (if overly bright) sprinkling of lights spread out below us.

The descending trail ends, to our relief, at the gate that separates the wild side of the park and the convent's back gate.

A street lamp at the corner of the parking lot casts a dim green light, as the door's shining knob turns itself incrementally, with the tiniest of creaks, opening inch by inch. I hold the door for Martie, scarcely breathing, then follow her into the convent, closing the door with meticulous trepidation. We tip toe down the deserted hallway, desperate to remain undetected. So far, so good.

At the foot of the stairs, we clasp hands in the silence and our eyes meet. Martie pulls her hand away for an awkward wave, leans to remove her shoes, then mouths, "good night," and heads quietly up the stairs.

I take a deep breath, turn into the empty unlit chapel, and grope my way to a seat. The flickering vigil light leaps about in the darkness, dancing a twisting and sinewy crimson I've never seen before.

Today's Woman

IT'S PRETTY WRENCHING. First, I grow up on a remote little prairie up north. Then off to a convent in California, a big-time state. Then teach as a nun in a parochial school in Oregon. What comes next? I've become more and more sure, each twilight as I scramble up Mount Tabor Park to look west over the city, sneak a few smokes, and think about it all: it's not my calling. My upcoming vows couldn't be heartfelt and true.

Anyway, with my style, I'd be caught doing one irregular thing or another—smoking cigarettes, playing raunchy rock and roll, drinking whisky, kissing women—and get thrown out anyway. I gave it my best shot—especially while chanting the Office with sunlight dancing through the stained-glass windows, or mustering little grade schoolers for a rousing chorus of "Three Little Piggies." But the habit doesn't fit.

As the teaching year ends at Assumption, I phone Sister Dorothy to set up my return to Mount Alverno within the week. She calls back to say that the following day her brother Michael will be driving down through Portland on his return from Seattle, and I can hitch a ride to California with him. Had we, she asks, met?

"Well, yes," I reply with a smile, "briefly."

H-m-m-m, okay. Red convertible will drive off with departing nun and dark-haired, gum-chewing, black tee-shirted young dude in aviator glasses. Another striking bit of unconventional. That night, I set about packing my few belongings and saying my goodbyes to the community and final Vespers and Compline in the little pink chapel.

After early breakfast, the red convertible stops by, and my guitar, suitcase, and I set off for California. Crossing Assumption's expanse of playground-parking lot, I turn back in the open car and wave to Sisters Martie and Gemma on the porch until we reach the street and take a left. We head toward the highway, take the on-ramp, and begin the journey south. Quickly the convertible hits freeway speed, and I grab my flailing veil for its premature removal before it flies off onto the roadside. Stashing it under the seat, I ride south all day long through Oregon and California with my very short haircut open to the blue sky.

On arrival at Mount Alverno at day's end, I re-veil, meet with Sister Dorothy, and tell her of my decision to leave for good. Sitting at her office desk, I look over her shoulder at the roses nodding in the patio window. Everything's blurry, as if it's not real. The *whoosh* of wind on the mountain passes still seems to be whipping around my ears. Sister Dorothy seems to be telling me how you set about to leave the convent and is arranging for me to meet with Mother Priscilla.

Following her instructions, I walk the long, shiny hallway and knock on the door at the Provincial office. My farewell conversation with Mother Priscilla isn't great.

"Unfortunately, Sister," she says, looking up at me from her desk, over her wire-rims, "your father neglected to pay your dowry when you entered." This is not good news. A dowry payment of $300 is customary when someone arrives to give the convent a try. It's meant to be returned if, down the road, you change your mind. That's all a novice brings to the new life she's entering, and all she'll take away if she chooses to leave. In other words, I haven't got a cent. Why didn't my dad do this for the convent— or for me? Ten minutes or so of uncomfortable hemming-and-hawing follows. Finally, Mother Priscilla unlocks and pulls open a desk drawer, hands me $75 in cash out of convent funds, and wishes me a lifetime of blessings. We say goodbye.

Pocketing the bills—the financial basis for my new life—I return down the hallway and arrange with Sister Dorothy for a ride into town. A few remaining possessions—knee socks, my copy of *Otter Fancies* by Starshine and a couple of other small books—go into my mostly empty suitcase, and I change into the old suit of my mother's that I arrived in three years ago. Within the hour, Stacy, a postulant I hardly know, drives me down the steep road off Mount Alverno to the bus station in the bustling town below.

Going all the way north to the prairie seems too complicated right now, and more of a past than a future—especially with my parents and the whole family in a shocked uproar because my next sister recently got pregnant without benefit of a husband. The City, which I know pretty well after studying and playing hooky at USF, seems a better place to begin. To start off, I can stay with a former-nun friend of Sister Gemma named Patricia, who lives out on Geary Street.

I clamber onto one of the hourly San Francisco-bound buses, suitcase in one hand, guitar and ticket in the other. Dazed, I find two seats together, one for me and one for my stuff. The door slams, and with a lurch, the Greyhound starts me on my journey as an ex-nun.

About halfway to the City, we stop in Millbrae. This morning I telephoned Margie, my Mount Alverno kitchen-pal of last year who had rescued the fawn with me before that. Margie left the convent a month or two ago, and now flies as a stewardess for United. Here she is at the Millbrae station, looking not a thing like a nun anymore and just the picture of an airline stewardess. Very smart and put together with spiffy clothes, a job, an apartment near the airport. Hey, maybe I can get something to wear besides my mom's old navy-blue suit!

"Not much use in it anymore," Mom had said, way back then as I readied to leave home. "Might as well take it to the convent."

Down the long aisle and out the bus door, I hustle with my guitar case in one hand, and mostly empty suitcase in the other, my ticket for the next bus stuffed in my jacket pocket. Margie gives me a hug. We grin and laugh a little. I've never left the convent before.

"I have." She smiles. "And it'll be fine." When I tell her my shopping idea, she's sure of it.

I glance at the schedule for next buses to the City—plenty of time. Off we go. Around the corner and across the street stands "Paisley Pastimes—*The* Complete Dress Shop for Today's Woman." Just the thing for two newly-ex-nuns. Margie in the lead and me scrambling behind with guitar and suitcase, we jaywalk across. Margie holds the door of the little shop as I navigate carefully so as not to topple any paisley dresses or shirts.

I spot just the thing, in plenty of paisley: black and grayish swirls swimming all over a soft, white, flowing dress. It will even go with my black knee socks and little-old-lady nun shoes.

The clerk comes up. She's older than us; all dressed up with bright pink lipstick and nail polish; wonders if we need some help. Margie quickly answers, "Yes. Thank you. We do." She has on lipstick and nail polish too. (I'm not sure I'll go that far.) "May we try that one?" She points toward the rack by the window to the silky dress that's got my eye.

"What sizes do you take?" the woman smiles at us.

"It's for my friend," Margie says and turns to me, her face crinkled up with the question. My fingers tighten on the guitar case and suitcase. Here I am in my mother's old blue suit, after the part of my life when she sewed all my clothes, and then three years of capacious brown nun robes. H-m-m-m-m—dress size? No idea.

Margie has to get back to work, gives a quick hug, and slips out the shop door. I'm in this alone. The clerk looks me over.

"How about a 10?" she says, handing me a dress, and directing me to a curtained cubicle where you try things on. It's a little cramped with me and the guitar and the suitcase and the dress.

Take off the worn blue skirt and top. Put on the dashing white and black and grayish paisley with its big sleeves and flowing skirt. No. Not at all as good a fit as my habit or even my mom's old suit. I don't even like the idea of leaving the curtained room wearing this tight little dress.

"How about one that's roomier?" I ask, poking my head around the purple-and-pink paisley curtain. Quickly, the dress returns in a 12. Still a bit snug. A 14 comes next. That's better. But I still think I'd like to feel those paisley sleeves flowing more and the skirt swooshing about my legs. Finally, a size 16 comes through the crack in the curtain.

I look across the room at the clock on the wall above the counter. Only fifteen minutes until the next bus leaves.

Put on the silky dress—nice loose sleeves and billowy skirt sashaying around my legs. There. That's about right. Quickly the blue suit folds into my suitcase, lined up next to the underwear, books, and knee socks. Fasten the lid. Buy the dress with $24.95 of the money Mother Priscilla gave me when I walked out of her office to say goodbye to life in the convent.

Run out the door in my spacious new dress. Cross the street. Lift my guitar and suitcase onto another Greyhound, and hand the driver my ticket. Making my way to the very back row, I sit next to my suitcase, get out my guitar.

"If you're going to San Fran-CIS-co, be sure you wear some flowers in your hair."

It's late afternoon. Just a few passengers sit here and there in the seats ahead of me, as we nose our way out of the station and head up to the Big City.

After-Song

Saint Teresa of Avila (1515-1582)—mystic, author, and founder of the Order of Discalced Carmelites in Spain—played guitar and composed songs for her community. Here is a concluding poem of hers as I have translated it from the Spanish and set it to be sung as a round.

Nada te turbe / Let Go Your Worry

Let Go Your Worry / Nada te turbe (4-part canon)
St. Teresa of Avila

Dianne Dugaw

Let go your wor-ry. Let go your fear. All trou-ble pas-ses, And God is near / here.
Na-da te tur-be. Na-da te espante. To-do se pa-sa. Dios no se muda.

Nada te turbe,   nada te espante.
Todo se pasa,   Dios no se muda.

Let go your worry,   let go your fear,
All trouble passes,   and God is near.
Let go your worry,   let go your fear,
All trouble passes,   and God is *here.*

Glossary of Terms

A COMPLEX, MANY-CENTURIES-OLD world of Roman Catholic belief and tradition is expressed in the practices that I followed, first in my family and then more elaborately in the 1960s convent. This list of terms mentioned in the stories here defines those that many readers may wish to know more about. (Terms in **boldface** are cross-referenced.)

Term	Meaning
Angelus	A devotion in honor of the Incarnation of Christ prayed in the morning, at noon, and in the evening and usually accompanied by the ringing of church bells.
antiphon	A short, devotional text, usually from the Bible, said or sung responsively.

Blessed Sacrament   The consecrated bread that, for Roman
                                  Catholics, is Christ's presence.

breviary   A book containing the service for the
                                  Hours of the **Divine Office** for each day, to
                                  be recited or sung by members of Roman
                                  Catholic **religious orders.**

Communion / Eucharist   The central act of **liturgical** worship in
                                  many Christian churches, also called the
                                  Mass, which celebrates the life, death, and
                                  resurrection of Jesus. The ritual enacts a meal
                                  patterned on his Last Supper with his
                                  disciples, in which bread and wine are
                                  consecrated and (in Roman Catholic
                                  belief) become his body and blood to be
                                  shared by the participants.

Divine Office   A **liturgical** service that is said or chanted
                                  at set times of the day in choir by religious
                                  communities (priests, monks, friars, nuns).
                                  The text consists of psalms, hymns, prayers,
                                  and appropriate readings contained in the
                                  breviary.

habit   Distinctive garb worn by members of
                                  religious orders, each with variations in
                                  color and style. Derived from medieval
                                  clothing, nuns' habits traditionally had a
                                  long tunic, a belt of cloth or rope, a
                                  scapular made of two strips of cloth joined

across the shoulders, and a veil. Somber
black, brown, and white were usual colors.

host

Unleavened bread cut in the form of a
wafer and used for the celebration of the
Eucharist in **Mass**. Once it is consecrated,
it becomes the Roman Catholic **Blessed
Sacrament.**

Hours

Times of day when sections of **Divine
Office** are recited, chanted, or read by
members of **religious orders.** They include
the "Greater Hours": matins (after mid-
night), lauds (morning), and vespers
(evening); and the "Lesser Hours" of prime,
terce, sext, none (mid-morning), and
compline (night).

litany

A prayer **liturgy** of supplications to God,
the saints, or the Blessed Virgin Mary, that
is said or chanted by an officiant as the
congregation answers with recurring
formulaic responses.

liturgy

A prescribed form for public religious ritual.
In the Roman Catholic Church, this
includes the **Divine Office** as well as the
sacraments including **Mass**, funerals, rites
for religious profession and the ordination
of priests, and consecration of churches,
objects, and sacred spaces. **Liturgy** follows

seasons of the year, annually commemorating the life of Jesus and feasts of the Blessed Virgin and the saints.

Mass

The Roman Catholic celebration of the **Eucharist**.

monasticism

A way of life apart from general society, to allow communion with the divine, governed by rules and customs regarding silence, prayer, liturgical ceremony, recreation, and work.

motherhouse

The central administrative house of a **religious order.**

Mother Superior

The administrator in charge of an entire **Order** of nuns, of a province and its convents, or of an individual convent.

novice

A person who has been admitted into a religious **order** and successfully passed a first period of probation as a **postulant**; a further trial period in the novitiate precedes taking vows and being **professed**.

Novice Mistress

A **professed sister** who is responsible for the training and governance of **novices**.

order

A term first applied in the 12th century to a religious community of monks, friars, or nuns based in a monastery, friary, or convent, whose members take vows after a probationary period and follow the rule of purpose and governance devised by a charismatic founder.

postulant

A person who wishes to become a member of a religious **order** and is in the first trial stage of admission.

Postulant Mistress

A **professed sister** who is responsible for the training and governance of **postulants**.

professed sister

A nun who has completed an order's entrance stages as **postulant** and **novice** (2–3 years) and taken vows to become a full member.

refectory

The dining hall of a religious community.

sacristy (sacristan)

A room adjoining a church or chapel where clergy put on their ritual vestments, and liturgical vessels and objects are stored. A **sacristan** looks after the room and makes necessary preparations for **liturgies**.

sanctuary

The section of a church or chapel that holds the high altar used for **Mass** and the tabernacle where the **Blessed Sacrament** is kept. Separated from the nave by altar-rails, the **sanctuary** is reserved for performance of **liturgy**.

sanctuary lamp

A candle generally in a red glass container, kept burning day and night wherever the **Blessed Sacrament** is kept.

scapular

An outer garment of a nun's **habit**, suspended from the shoulders, symbolizing the commitment to live according to the ideals and rule of the order.

seminarian

A student in a seminary, especially of the Roman Catholic Church, studying to become a priest.

transubstantiation

A Catholic doctrine which holds that, in the **Eucharist**, the substance of the bread and wine is converted into the substance and presence of the Body and Blood of Christ.

typology

This complex system of correspondences understands the Hebrew and Christian parts of the bible to be a unified account of a divine plan for salvation, in which elements in the Hebrew bible forecast, and are more fully revealed in, the life of Jesus and in the doctrines, practices, and **liturgies** of Christianity.

Acknowledgments

I AM DEEPLY GRATEFUL to Schaffner Press and Tim Schaffner for choosing my manuscript for this award in memory of Nicholas Schaffner, musician and author. It is an honor to be in such company.

Many writers and editors have prompted, questioned, shaped, and polished my words along the way. Thank you, Anne Dubuisson, developmental editor extraordinaire, for helping me find just what *California Medieval* wanted to say. Then, gratitude and blessings to our "Wicked Good Writing Group" here in Eugene, Oregon—Amanda Powell, Karen McPherson, Kit Sibert, Mary Wood, and Shannon Applegate—wonderful writers and colleagues whose readings have improved this book at every stage. Likewise, thank you to Jayne Lewis and Suzanne Simons for your readings and encouragement, and to Frank Hesketh for heartening words as well as photographic wizardry. My thanks to Elizabeth Howard—former student, colleague, and whimsical website prompter. And to Terry McQuilkin for help in formatting the score. Appreciation goes as well to Abigail Welhouse—poet and more than a publicist.

I am forever grateful to my parents: Dr. Bill, my father, for his wacky kids' songs, and Donna, my mother, for her singing and playing. As a toddler I observed our Baldwin spinet piano marking our family values: it was our living room's only furniture for a good long while. And to Father Joseph and Cousin Sister Judy, beloved family models of inspirited generosity, learning, faith, laughter, and verve.

Thank you to all who have sparked my music-making, especially Sister Marie Celine, and of course my parents and siblings who suffered my piano practice at even the earliest hours of the day. Later on, kind and inspired Dr. William Kearns flexibly fostered my one-of-a-kind graduate work in Music School, prairie-raised musical semi-autodidact that I was. And of course, this book could not exist without the cavalcade of encouraging (and sometimes obstructing) Franciscan sisters in our little prairie school and later: Sisters Angela, Marietta, Martha, Wilma, and on and on—women of good humor, resilience, and faith with no nonsense. And in recent years, Victoria McMillan, wise champion and counselor in all things.

Then, I look back with appreciation on a lifetime of beloved pianos and organs of various sorts, a host of guitars and banjos, as well as harmonicas, penny whistles, recorders, and marimbas in diverse ranges and keys.

And finally, my deepest heartfelt thanks to my beloved spouse Amanda, who long ago responded to my stories, "Why don't you write about that, honey?" She has generously heard and thought and read and edited my words at every step, and I cannot imagine it any other way.

And of course, thanks and a little biscuit to my canine consulting editor, wee Kinnikinnik.

Thank you, thank you all of you.

Dianne Dugaw is a singer-musician, writer, and scholar who publishes in folklore, music, and literary studies with an emphasis on queer topics. Her childhood on a small Pacific Northwest ranch and her early years as a Catholic nun shape her storytelling and scholarship. Her books, which include *Warrior Women & Popular Balladry* (University of Chicago Press) and *'Deep Play'—John Gay & the Invention of Modernity* (University of Delaware Press), investigate cross-dressing women heroes, ballad origins of musical comedy, and gender and sexuality in history. She has also recorded two CDs, singing traditional British and American folksongs. Professor Emerita at the University of Oregon, Dugaw lives in the Willamette Valley with her wife and wee dog.